Death Row:
An Affirmation of Life

COMPILED & EDITED BY STEPHEN LEVINE

WITH THE ASSISTANCE OF DOVIE C. MATHIS,
A- 84403, DEATH ROW, SAN QUENTIN

AND THE INSPIRATION OF JACK RAINSBERGER,
7588, DEATH ROW, NEVADA STATE PRISON

GLIDE PUBLICATIONS, SAN FRANCISCO

Cover painting "Crucifixion" by Dion Wright.

International Standard Book Number: 0-912078-12-7
Library of Congress Catalog Card Number: 72-176239

© *1972 by Glide Publications, 330 Ellis Street, San Francisco 94102*

Photographs on pp. 36, 60, 86, 98, 112, 124, 172, & 182 are
© *1971 by Steve Kahn and may not be reprinted without prior*
permission in writing from photographer and publisher

Photograph p. 2 courtesy of Prentice-Hall, Inc.
Photograph p. 140 United Press International
Photo of Death Row, San Quentin, courtesy of the San Francisco Chronicle

*To three-year-old daughter Tara, by whose light,
and despite whose help, this book was produced.*

Contents

Acknowledgments

MANY THANKS:

To Nick Harvey, Ruth Gottstein and Donald Kuhn for generating the energy at Glide Publications which saw this long-thought-of project come to fruition.

To Ruth McLane, who absorbed so much of the emotional slag which the purifications of this undertaking brought forth while she typed the manuscript, for participating with me in the sorrows and joys of which this book is composed.

To Blanche Bontempi, who introduced me to Dovie Mathis, opening the gates of San Quentin prison.

To Cathy Kornblith of Connections, who transmitted a germ of consciousness.

To Paul Halvonik, Doug Lyons, Jack Himmelstein, Ed Morgan, Marshal Krause, Fred Kilbride, Cyril Ash, Sam Lionel, Michael Kennedy, Michael Marcus, Sarita Waite, Robert Herr, Dennis DeNaut, and all the other attorneys who helped gain information and lent their personal support to this book during the many years of preparation and formal compilation.

To Steve Kahn, for his cooperation and photographic insight.

To Betsy Klein, whose nit-picking helped in various stages along the way.

To the Eldridge Foundation, for their support and encouragement from the start.

To Jan Marinissen, Criminal Justice Secretary for the Northern California regional office of the American Friends Service Committee (Quakers), who appraised the work in manuscript and was always available when a bit of information was required, just as the Quakers are so often present in prisons when help is needed. (The Quakers are to the prison system what the Red Cross is to disaster victims.)

And to the many who aided in so many ways in seeing the book completed: Mary Vangi, Ron Polte, Walter Bowart, Craig Caughlan, Peter Zimels, Beverly Cox of the Garberville Public Library, and those whose names do not come to mind at this writing.

And most of all to Patricia, my wife, who shared with me so many sleepless nights and intense mornings.

And peace to all sentient beings.

Foreword

In the midst of poetry I encountered Death Row. While editing the life-affirming slightly psychedelic *San Francisco Oracle* in 1967, I was introduced to Jack Rainsberger via a mutual friend. At the time, Jack had been on Death Row at the Nevada State Prison in Carson City for nearly ten years. The intense interface of our letters and visits from either side of Life Row has grown and, in the nearly four years since our first contact, has become this book.

The work progressed very slowly and organically. Because the San Francisco Bay area was so close, it developed that those men with whom I had the deepest communication, the greatest opportunity to visit, were in San Quentin, two hundred miles south of where we live beside the Eel River near Garberville, California. My monthly trips to the city became my monthly trips to Death Row.

It was at San Quentin that I found the archetype for all prisons. This is understandable; California has the largest prison system in what is referred to as the "free world," and more men under sentence of death than any other state in the nation. At the time of this writing (September 1971) there are ninety-five men and four women condemned to death in this state.

I do not think this book could have been done so completely at any other place, at any other time. In the beginning of the project I had thought of contacting men whom I knew had been on various Death Rows in other parts of the country such as Paul Crump in Illinois, John Brady in Maryland, William Maxwell in Arkansas, Arthur Davis in Connecticut, and spokesmen for clear thinking such as Karl Menninger, Ramsey Clark, and Robert Lindner. But as it came to pass, this book was to be more personal than that, and the closeness to San Quentin turned out to be but one more aspect of the "divine providence" by which the work was completed.

It is difficult to imagine that even if I should be overtaken by amnesia I could ever forget the men I have met while compiling this book. That several life-long friendships have grown out of a book about Death Row is but one of the many ironies which have become the life-affirming heartbeat of the work. Through extensive exchanges of letters and personal visits, I have been in contact with each of these men except Edgar Smith. His location in the Death House in Trenton, New Jersey, and his present necessity to work on his case preclude direct communication. Edgar is caught on the second hand of legal justice; we hold our breath and wait.

As the book neared completion there were moments when the mind could go nowhere but to the dying of these men. Crickets, the slow turbine of night, whirring beside the dark window. Peace just beyond. Yet there in death with these men there was a quietude. An involuntary centering on dissolution. A great sadness which putting into words now mocks: an indescribable interlocking, an interchangeability, like replaceable parts of an ongoing vehicle, as if none of us were totally free of this retribution of fate; as if each of us were somehow on Death Row merely by having been born into the human form. There were moments of bewilderment as to the real meaning of this work, times of great sadness at my brothers' condition (both captive and keeper), and the joy that the human spirit could surmount even these incredible hardships.

In February, four months after the formal compilation had begun, our son Noah came forth to the coordinated breathings of a natural birth, "the cervix stretched to allow heaven to pass," his birth demagnetizing the sometimes overwhelming effects of working so close to despair and unrequited hope. It was a reflection of the rebirth of those I was meeting and coming to know, just as our first child's birth three years before had come in the midst of the production of Jack Rainsberger's book. Consistently, it seems, a consciousness of death breeds a consciousness of life. The cycle is unending—a continuum of light into dark into light.

Death Row: An Affirmation of Life

Introduction

This is not a book against capital punishment. It is not a book *against* anything, other than the drowsy blindness which separates each of us from his fellow beings. Capital punishment all too clearly personifies this separateness.

This book is an attempt at repairing our ability to see and experience life. The best it might do is act as a sort of emotional and spiritual braille by which we define our state of mind. It rises from that point where life and death meet.

This is a book of affirmation, a collection of the writings that reaffirm and demonstrate life from those most aware of its fateful meaning, by those most aware of what the taking of life results in in the mind. These are the writings of hard and prolonged introspection. They are the sounds of the soul struggling to make it back to the surface. They are the healing chants, prayers, confessions, exorcisms, percolations, ego tales, fantasies, visions, and love songs of the condemned. They are a part of us all.

Each man in this book uniquely conveys a state of mind which at one time or another has been common to everyone. These are archetypal phases of consciousness. They vary from a search for justice to a search for the silent self, from a desire to be free to a hope for a quick and merciful death. Each is a chronicle of personal growth and fulfillment. Together they are the works of the self-educated, the expanding, the reborn, and the hopeful. There is, ironically, probably more hope on Death Row than in any place of similar size in the world.

Each of these men is accused of murder. Each has found a new life within. Each deserves to live.

We are all and each capable of murder. It is a possibility pro-
grammed in our genes. It is a residue of our biologic make-up
born of a few million years of evolution. How many thought
forms might the saber-toothed beast of the dark underdream
take in each of us? Who among us can say that under no circumstances would he take the life of another? Who is without anger? Who is not defensive of his imagined self? Who
has not wished for the demise of one he felt obstructed his happiness? Who has not had that awful daydream of death, or killed
himself in fantasy?

Murder is a moral concept, not an action. It is something for
which we are supposed to be legally responsible. The million
deaths of God-loves-only-us religious wars (as all wars are
religious wars) fought in the fictitious name of higher causes
apparently are excusable, necessary. It is just the way one
looks at it whether or not the slaying of one being by another is
actually murder rather than a commendable form of heroism
or patriotism or some other sense of duty by which we crush
the life out of one of our fellow beings. The executioner certainly isn't a murderer, nor is the Medal of Honor winner, nor
the policeman protecting those particular molecules we call
property, nor the inattentive surgeon, nor the unhearing judge
nor the ambitious district attorney, nor the careless driver, nor
he who thoughtlessly tosses a lit cigarette from a car into tin-
derbox forests firing towns and campsites, roasting all life in
an unconscious path. Nor is there of course guilt by complicity,
the waving of flags, the building of fences, the support of the
death penalty. All those are innocent according to The Word—
man's law. But the man who is so off center and blind with his
own pain that he kills a loved one, or in the throes of the socially accepted hunger for material wealth, panics and pulls the
momentary trigger—this man is a murderer.

More have been slaughtered in the name of God than in any
other cause. None of these of course is murder. Nor did we
murder thousands by the firebombings of Frankfurt and Dres-
den a few years ago. Certainly the yellow flesh of ten thousand

children burning in the jungles of Viet Nam is not murder, nor is the suicide-inducing glance of hate, nor the slavery of the black, nor the fascism of our loves. These I am told are all excusable. But the murderer who breaks the law must be punished, though he may have approached the end of his sorrow, his own death, with the death of another. In Dante's cosmic hell, the murdered turned to the murderer and said, "What hast thou done; I am thyself."

Albert Camus, winner of the 1957 Nobel Peace Prize, speculated throughout his lifetime on the validity of executing a man for a crime he'd committed in the past. Since the mind is constantly fluctuating, the man we condemn changes from killer to victim between his crime and our punishment.

Furthermore, the death penalty, originally instituted as a deterrent to future criminals, has failed (in every instance) to reduce the number of murderers in any society. The spectacle of public executions proved so abhorrent to the civilized community that it is now done secretly by the state with no witness but the priest and the hangman.

In his essay "Reflections on the Guillotine," Camus contended that capital punishment failed to hold murderers in check,

> because the instincts warring in man are not as the law claims, constant forces in a state of equilibrium. They are variable forces, waxing and waning, and their repeated lapses from equilibrium nourish the life of the mind as electrical oscillations, when close enough, set up a current. Just imagine the series of oscillations, from desire to lack of appetite, from decision to renunciation, through which each of us passes in a single day. Such lapses from equilibrium are generally too fleeting to allow a single force to dominate the whole being. But it may happen, that one of the soul's forces breaks loose until it fills the whole field of consciousness. . .and at such a moment, no instinct, not even life itself, can oppose the tyranny of that irresistible force. For capital punishment to be really intimidating human nature would have to be different; it would have to be as stable and serene as the law itself . . . But then human nature would be dead.

Some reading this book might feel themselves incapable of murder. But this is the comfortable state of mind of one with book in familiar surroundings. Could that same mind in that same man in other surroundings, under other pressures, with other tensions say the same thing; would he be capable of thinking the same way? We are each and all capable of murder; only the circumstances, inordinate to be sure, must be present for the same reaction: the quick unconscious spasm of the trigger finger, the slaughter of something we would see destroyed in ourselves, the very real though symbolic murder of another for our own inadequacy. Yet how is a man who wishes an end to his anguish to be released by being sacrificed? Why do we perpetrate the standard by which man kills by condoning his execution? Is not capital punishment a sick way of condoning the actions of the murderer? Aren't we saying in essence to this man that under certain circumstances it is advisable to kill that which we find despicable? Aren't we in a horribly unconscious way forgiving him his act by committing murder on the murderer?

The murderer in a way selects a scapegoat for his own painful state of mind just as the state recreates that same scapegoat consciousness by selecting for death a personification of its own ills. Just as the murderer might kill another for the traits he despises in himself, the state executes the murderer for manifesting those traits which it finds unbearable in itself.

The state elects to maintain the least conscious response to the unconsciousness of others. But why must the state react at the lowest possible level? Why doesn't it choose understanding as its means of dealing with its own problems? Is not the state itself, in killing another, committing its own suicide? Could it not show greater compassion to those whom it has nurtured, to that within itself with which it refuses to identify? How is blindness cured by plucking the eyes from the sightless? The state kills its strays to keep the herd tight.

What the state does is analogous to snipping loose threads from an unraveling seam to continue to make the threadbare garment seem quite neat and new. It fools no one. Capital punishment presages the decay and measures the death glut of the societies that maintain it. The irony is that any one of us might be reading this a year from now on Death Row. Who among us is sane enough for execution?

III

Before the colosseum "games" of ancient Rome the condemned gladiators stood before the royal podium and said: "We who are about to die salute you, Caesar." But the men who have written this book do not have that immediacy of struggle or that intimacy with foe Death on the field of battle. These are the lives of those who must face death because of the wording of a legal appeal or the capriciously bad stomach of a judge or juror. They are not condemned for murder, for then there would be thousands on Death Row, men who have committed similar crimes under similar circumstances but who have been given lesser sentences. They are the arbitrarily dead.

We execute for the man, not for the crime. We execute for heresy, for a different way of looking at things. We execute geographically, sentencing one man to his death for an act which if committed in another state might not be similarly punishable. We execute by mores, by the unwritten acculturation of society. A drooping eyelid into which we might pour our darkest fantasies is enough to evoke the penalty of death. An accent, a limp, a defiant attitude, a defensive response at being forced to plead for one's life; we execute for being too different.

We execute not for the crime but for the traits of the individual found guilty. If he is black, young, uneducated, poor, esoteric in his religious or spiritual leanings, outspoken, or slightly deformed he has a better chance of getting the death sentence than if he is white, middle-class, hard-working, an upholder of the two-party system and scared. The jury seldom condemns itself. It is the foreign, the different, the heretical whom their compassion seldom reaches. We tend to be more lenient with those with whom we can identify. Has any murderer ever really been heard by a jury of his peers?

How much of each of us resides on Death Row? Is Life Row as distant from Death Row as one might have imagined? Is the mind of the murderer so different from our own? Or is it that the Original Sin from which we all suffer is an abstract feeling of guilt, extending from the violence of toilet training to the myths of masturbation? Have we not all been chided as children not to lie and not to steal, as though each of us were the only person in human history ever to follow those very natural inclinations? But who among us was told *how* not to lie, and *how* not to steal? We have been instilled with a distrust of our own natural motivations. We are suppressed as growing organisms, confused, creating a deep feeling that we are all abnormal, that each of us is somehow "odd." Is this not the reason why so many of us struggle to accomplish an integration with society as an arbitrary repository for our feelings of unnatural inadequacy, for our ambushed desires for acceptance and approbation? Is this not the means by which every military death-dealing state has maintained grace? We execute for not adhering or relating to that unnamed guilt within. We execute those who personify that which we most fear in ourselves: that which we believe is most unnatural, that which we care least to face and deal with. In a peculiar way we execute for our own fear that we too might be the murderer before us. We execute to extirpate from our external environment that which we dare not see within. We break the mirror which horrifies us; we crush the skull which holds that which we too, under certain circumstances, might manifest. We show ourselves no compassion; we in essence never forgive ourselves for that point in evolution at which we find ourselves still capable of murder.

Yet the real unnaturalness in this tribal exorcism we call legal execution is the way in which we reap our vengeance— the way in which we punish ourselves for our inherited capability of murder, clearly expressed in the death penalty. We as a species are on trial. Though so many quote the Old Testament incantation "an eye for an eye, a tooth for a tooth," we take both eyes for an eye; we take the whole throat in payment for that tooth. We do not simply kill for killing; we instead torture with years of an unnatural, maddening environment and then kill for what may have been but a single uncontrolled instant in a man's life. The emotions of the murderer tossed him beyond life sufficiently to enable him to kill another, yet we react to this with the unnatural deliberation of a Grand Inquisitor or a Mad Scientist. We add an element of torture; we underline the unnaturalness of our act by not responding immediately and in the present as did the murderer. We sentence this man to a prolonged confrontation with death and a torturously slow means of execution.

We are life and only by an affirmative pro-life recognition shall we ever decrease the amount of aggression and murder that occurs. All must revere life, not just the accused. The judge and jury too must set the precedent that life is sacred though often painful.

IV

Death Row is a unique environment. There is a consciousness of death which occurs in no other place to such a degree. The condemned are constantly reminded of a fixed moment when their lives may be terminated. Most have experienced the "last twenty-four hours" more than once. Most have felt slow-eyed Death approach only to be cast off once more by the actions of a writ or a compassionate judge's temporary stay of execution. Each has in some way been involved with the death of another, whether by actual commission or by an innocent complicity with fate. For there are the guilty and the innocent awaiting their demise side by side, each deprived the opportunity afforded others of denying the inevitability of death. Death Row for each is a meditation on life.

There is little difference between the best death rows and the worst; it is just a matter of degree. From what was Death Row in Arkansas (until Rockerfeller in a final *beau geste* commuted all condemned) to the relative opulence of San Quentin in California is just a difference in the technology of death. Once, when reading about the conditions at the Arkansas State Prison's Death Row, I was surprised to find that each man was provided with a hot plate in his cell—something I thought was a bit of enlightened compassion, only to find later that this was because they were not provided food and it was expected that they would acquire their own if they cared to eat. How little difference, though, from what is considered one of the best "rows": San Quentin's, replete with TV, phonographs, meals served in the cells, a few hours of exercise or an occasional visit and nearly open regulations on letter writing. Still death is there. Often, as I waited to see a contributor to this book, the man was brought down the long hall backing the visiting room flanked front and back by guards who called to all who might hear: "Clear the way, dead man coming, dead man coming."

Death Row is a unique environment. Its monotony and repetitious predictability create to varying degrees a ritualistic sensory deprivation environment: the constant beige flat hard steel, the endless rows of rivet heads protruding like the tiny helmets of buried soldiers in a battlefield cemetery, the constancy of iron bars, the grey concrete. Rather than being bombarded as in any other contemporary twentieth century American environment, the eye* wanders seeking stimuli, escape. Death Row creates a withdrawal of the senses, an inward turning, a necessity to self-stimulate, to remain centered, to keep from slipping off into bizarre fantasies of persecution and dull-eyed madness, to keep the mind intact.

Stimuli are at a premium. Each seeks to compensate for this sensory starvation in his own way. Some pace humming. Some do push-ups. Some play chess or gamble for cigarettes at cards. Some listen to a few old songs together, remembering the clearer skies of the past. Others sit quietly at solitaire, moving with the even precision of a diamond cutter over each facet of a newly turned card. Many read Zane Grey and Jack London. Some visit with Goethe or Kant. Some read comic books. There are those who sit motionless at midnight attempting to discover the intrinsically pure essence of mind. A few draw or write, paint or pray.

All share to some degree the sensory input of television. In San Quentin, the death row with which I am most familiar, a television set is provided against the far wall for each three cells. A remote control tuner is situated above each bunk; selection of programs is worked out within each group of three men. I have read letters by men considered "rabid beasts" (by those who use such extravagant incantations against life) explaining with great care why they prefer "I Love Lucy" to "Bonanza." Men have been stabbed for attempting to "rip off" a favorite program. Those most attuned to themselves attempt to elude the ever prevalent addictions that they see about them, closely regulating the amount of time they allow for television to keep the mind from becoming a comic book caricature of what it might be; to enjoy television without becoming it. Television, as Frank Lloyd Wright put it, is chewing gum for the eyes. But to a man deprived of stimuli it may mean a last grip on sanity itself.

For those unwilling to drown in this atmosphere, self-education is a means of bringing the mind to attention: to keep from becoming, as one writer put it, "borderline vegetables"; to ward off the "basket case" consciousness into which so many disappear.

One of the first studies of men who find creativity a survival mechanism on Death Row, after their ironic recognition of "reason" in their survival study of the intricate latticework of law, is mathematics. Mathematics becomes an attempt to induce some concrete logic into their environment and lives. Often it is followed by the study of general semantics, in an attempt to gain control of the way the mind goes out and attaches emotional reaction (meaning) and response to various emotionally laden key words and ideas. It is also at this point that foreign languages are often taken up. These are the attempts at freeing oneself from the overpowering motivations of the past in an aim at centering in the Death Row present without vegetating or going totally mad. It is all an attempt to gain control of the wild ramblings of the mind, to rein in the vehicle of their lives, to lead themselves instead of being led as they may have been in the past. It is an attempt at last to bring fate under control. This sensory deprivation environment breeds insight in some and decaying boredom in others; it is creativity for some, deterioration for others.

The forced contemplation of one's own demise, at times recognized through the previous destruction of another, creates a unique mental environment as well. How many of us know the exact time at which they will die? How many know how they will die—and who will be their murderers? The Death Row environment is unique because there is very little chance that a man there will die by any other means than those prescribed by the state. There will be no accidental drownings in a bathtub, no slipping down stairs, no automobile mishaps. The condemned are protected against chance. Death Row is an intensive care environment culminating in execution.

Only the "lucky" gain much from it. This is a book of the "lucky ones": those who have kept hold of their sanity and somehow managed to grow within this uniquely inorganic environment. They often speak with the voices of whole men. But they are not the average. They are the gifted, those who have somehow "caught hold" of themselves. But there are the others too for whom this book must speak: the illiterate, the insane, the world-weary and the broken; those unable to concentrate their cries to written language, incapable of making themselves understood, facing an inner and outer reality so different from our own that it is incommunicable, so uncommon and painful is their vision. And there are the others: the dismally mute, the waiting.

v

This book is the record of an experience. It is the record of each contributor's mind as well as of my relationship to the mind of each contributor. It has been written by the men themselves. I have only been the lens through which their energies were focused.

It was a book ready to be done. It underlines the absurdity of our age at a time when this absurdity is becoming more self-evident to a growing number of people. It is a product of its times. It could not have been done a year ago. A year ago writers in San Quentin's Death Row were not allowed to send out manuscripts (a post-Chessman restriction). Even at present it would be impossible: after the bloody Saturday of 21 August 1971, in which six died, all "unauthorized reporters" have been excluded from entry into San Quentin. But Death Row, like any environment, changes; privileges come and go like newspaper headlines. A year from now, if the Supreme Court decides that execution is not "cruel and unusual punishment," many of these men will probably have been put to death. And killing will go on as usual and we will not have "given peace a chance." We will not have trusted that which is life within us any more than the murderer did at the time of murder. If executions resume, we will echo the death rattle of the original victim, allowing each deadly bullet in every stick-up panic-killing to continue to ricochet, blindly killing more and more.

Knowing that one tends to become what he opposes I do not intend this book to be an assault on the injustice of torturing and killing the killer. The forces of unconsciousness, the vehemence of those who cry out for the death penalty is so great that to involve oneself in their state of mind is to somewhere poison oneself. I have experienced this toxification more than once during these years' work. These death wishers kill themselves with hate. Their confusion as to what life is all about is a great contagion; it is better to stay on the side of life than to enter across into their dark consciousness. By understanding that which is destruction within each of us, we come to understand that which is creativity. In a hope that we may find peace in our hearts, this meditation on Death Row is offered as a reaffirmation of life.

Caryl Chessman

CARYL CHESSMAN personifies to many the predicament of the condemned. His best-selling books of the 1950s brought world attention to his fight for life. During his record-setting twelve years on San Quentin's Death Row (at a time when the average length of time between sentencing and execution was under two years) he used every legal means available to gain a retrial on charges of which he claimed to be innocent— charges which no longer carry the death penalty. He was executed on 2 May 1960 at 10:10 a.m.

Trial by Ordeal

Caryl Chessman

You're assured of enough to eat. You can keep clean and warm.

But you have no privacy. Day and night, you're watched closely. Having claimed it, the state is jealous of your life. Every possible safeguard is taken to prevent you from cheating the executioner—by digging, cutting or assaulting your way to stolen freedom; by self-destruction; by fleeing to the world of the insane. You've come to the wrong place if curious eyes and the probing beams of flashlights make you uneasy.

A condemned man's nights are long and often sleepless. It is during the deep silences of the prison night that his past returns to be relived. It is then that he examines his life and necessarily comes to know something of himself. How much he learns depends upon his nature and the nature of his quest.

Life on the Row is a blending of the real and the unreal; it's a clash of internal and external tension, the tension of everyday living magnified a hundred times. You're a prisoner in a strange land. You are and you aren't a part of the larger whole around you. You form friendships and your friends die. You dream and your dreams die.

"He," says Michaux, "who wants to escape the world translates it." So, paradoxically, does he who is doomed and who wants to escape back *into* the world, the world of warmth and love and purpose. But his translations often are terrible rationalizations, offered in a language only he understands. As

From the book *Trial by Ordeal* by Caryl Chessman. © 1955 by Caryl Chessman. Reprinted with permission of the publisher, Prentice-Hall, Inc., Englewood Cliffs, New Jersey.

in a nightmare, he cries out and no one hears him. He is brave and his bravery is in vain. He runs but he must run in circles. In desperation, he seeks to return to the peace of the womb but he is forced, instead, to plunge forward and downward toward a cold, limitless darkness.

He does the best he can with the mental and spiritual equipment he has. With hate or humor he parodies his existence. He lives from day to day. He learns to ascribe no importance to himself. Yet he remains all important to himself, for when oblivion claims him, devours him, it will be claiming and devouring his nightmare world as well. Total philosophic annihilation of self's universe is the inevitable end-product when this universe is a contracting prison that denies meaning to self.

On Death Row life not only copies art, it creates a grotesque art form all its own that makes life its slave, death its master.

In many respects, my existence in this house of death has been atypical. I have spent a longer time here than any other man ever has. For five years and ten months I personally handled the litigation of the case in the appellate courts without assistance; whether I lived or died hinged entirely on the legal moves I made, the documents I filed. I still must make all final decisions in my struggle for survival.

A year after my arrival, the prison officials approved my converting one of the Row cells, No. 2437, into a sort of office in which I might do my legal work.

Crowded always by the place, I've learned to hold Death Row at a distance, but I've learned the hard way. If some mixed-up character wants to whistle at midnight or make like Gene Krupa on his table at three o'clock in the morning, well, let him have his fun. If another guy feels he has to swagger around and let it be known how double tough he is, fine.

I've acted out my anxiety, first with fists and hatred, now with words and a generative faith. I've had my bellyful of violence. I know there's not any glamour in being doomed or being on Death Row. On the other hand, I refuse to cringe. I think I still have the right to hold my head up. I know that ninety percent of those citizens who are always giving me hell would be rather sorry specimens after spending a few months in my situation. But this gives me no special pleasure. If one of them should happen to wind up on the Row I'd doubtless do my best to help the poor guy in any way I could.

I've developed outside interests. I'm as keenly concerned with the young lives of two small friends as I am with my own. I've learned to love and to know the meaning of friendship and I'm not ashamed of it. I have ten approved correspondents on my mailing and visiting list, the maximum number allowed. I've kept up with the world beyond this tiny, violent one around me. Someday I hope to be a part of that larger world again.

And yet I am a strange guy, for my hope embraces more than a desire merely to put Death Row behind me. After the years I've spent here I would never be content until I knew the place itself, grim and dreary and forbidding, no longer existed at all. I've experienced too much, I've seen and heard and felt too much to feel otherwise.

Once, shortly after my arrival, I almost lost my mind. Once I nearly committed suicide. More than once I was on the verge of saying to hell with it; survival wasn't worth *this*. More than once I've been in savage brawls. More than once I found myself in the special disciplinary cells, with only hate for company.

I've witnessed the disintegration of the minds of the men around me. I've seen these men naked on the floor, rolling in their own excrement. I've listened as they smashed and shattered the sinks and toilets and fixtures in their cells. I've watched them savagely attack one another. I've heard their prayers and their screams and their curses. I've observed their bodies being removed after they had destroyed themselves. I've read their pathetic pleas for mercy.

I've marveled, too, at their courage, their sense of humor,

their dignity. I've been glad for their friendship. With them, I've known a loneliness that is indescribable...

[I recall when] the executioner claimed [a] friend, Sandy, a quiet youngster who was executed after barely reaching his majority. Day after day we'd walked away the recreational period together, laughing, joking, discussing every subject under the sun—and then, suddenly, he was gone. It was hard to believe; it didn't make sense. And my resentment at his destruction played a trick on me.

I was transferred one night from the legal cell to Cell 2455, my home, and began reading a newsmagazine. In the art section I discovered an article about Vincent Van Gogh, in whom Sandy and I both had had a keen interest. Without thinking, I called out:

"Hey, Sandy!"

No answer.

I tried again. "Hey, Sandy! Wake up! What are you trying to do, sleep your life away?"

Then I remembered. Sandy was dead. The executioner had put him to sleep for keeps.

That is what life on Death Row is like. One day you're alive and the next day you aren't. The next day you're a body in a morgue. The next day, between ten-twenty and eleven a.m., the men who are waiting their turn will hear the phone bell in the sergeant's office jangle. The sergeant will call to the floor officer. He will tell him the execution is over. The floor officer will go to the dead man's cell, accompanied by the prisoner who does cleanup work on the Row, remove the dead man's personal effects and bedding, place these on a rubber-tired utility cart. The cart will be wheeled out; the cell will be scrubbed, depersonalized. The next day, the next week or the next month a new arrival will be brought to the Row and assigned the cell.

The cycle will be repeated. Death will keep interrupting life. The doomed will go on living from day to day until, abruptly, individually or in pairs, their lives will be canceled out. A few, of course, will get away. They will be granted new trials or their death sentences will be commuted to life imprisonment. So hope always dies hard. . . .

II

On the Row at the present time we have, according to no less an authority than the newspapers:

1. Two "fiends" and three "monsters"
2. One "moon-mad killer"
3. One "cold-eyed, cold-blooded" leader of a "Mountain Murder Mob"; his alleged triggerman, "The Weasel"
4. One "sex-crazed psychopathic beast"
5. Me
6. An assortment of "vicious," "sneering," "leering," "brutal" and "kill-crazy" murderers, plus a former private eye turned "diabolical" kidnapper.

As the papers and "true" detective magazines tell it, we're creatures on the lam from Hell. Satan, in one of his most satanic moments, blew life into the figures on display in some sinister waxworks of horrors and *presto!* there we were.

Here we are, an inhuman assemblage. Or so you are led to believe.

Fiction is no alibi for truth, and certainly is a dangerous substitute for it. Newspapers and newsmagazines especially should realize this. They are, with the help of some prosecuting and judicial agencies, the monster-makers of our time. They create a demand and then cater to it with a mass-produced product, machine-tooled and phony.

Let me illustrate. Bill Cook emerged from a nightmare childhood and a prison term broke and friendless. He was in his early twenties. He was short and squat, and one of his eyelids drooped. There was no warmth in him, no feeling of belonging. He was on his own in a world he regarded as hostile. He got a gun, returned to crime, petty stuff. Crime put him on the run. In making a getaway he kidnaped a family taking a trip in their car. He warned them not to signal for help. In passing through a small town one of the older children saw an officer and began shouting for help. The bodies of the family

9

were found in an abandoned mine. Bill had slain them. One of the greatest manhunts in the history of the country was launched.

Bill made his way to California. The body of a salesman whose car Bill had taken was found in a southern California desert. The hunt for him was intensified. He was caught, finally, in Mexico, after having kidnaped two campers and taken them with him as hostages. Tried by the federal government for the kidnaping of the slain family, he was sent to Alcatraz for three hundred years. Unsatisfied, California brought him to trail for the killing of the salesman. He was speedily doomed.

Two days before Bill was executed here in San Quentin's gas chamber a California daily of large circulation published one of those breathless horror stories that are so common. Part of it read:

"He [Warden Harley Teets] called Cook 'the strangest killer we have ever had in Condemned Row. He is surly and belligerent and refuses to have anything to do with anyone. The longest speech he made was on the day he arrived. I greeted him with "Hello, Bill" and he just snarled back, "You can go to hell."'

"The other twenty condemned killers in the Row regard Cook as a monster, Teets said. 'Not only do they refuse to talk to him but they even clam up when guards try to get them to talk about him,' the warden said. 'The idea of a man murdering a whole family is unusual even in this place,' said Teets, 'and the men have no use for him.'

"Cook has gained twenty-five pounds since he has been in the death house and spends most of his time reading Zane Grey books. He follows the printed lines with a forefinger and moves his lips when he reads."

The remarkable thing about that story is that so much hooey could be compressed into such a small space. I know the warden didn't say what he is quoted as saying. Putting handy words in a prison official's mouth is an old stunt, but how cynical and hypocritical and brazen can you get when reporting "news"? The truth is that we did not consider Cook a monster; as far as we were concerned he was just another guy. We got along with him and he got along with us quite well.

Bill Cook wasn't fond of authority; neither was he aggressively belligerent or defiantly surly. As a matter of fact, he never once had trouble with any of the other condemned men, nor was he ever charged with a violation of prison rules. During exercise period he mingled with the rest of us. I had more than one long talk with him. He read all sorts of books without benefit of pointing finger or moving lip and on the subject of geography, his passion, he was unquestionably well informed.

I'm not suggesting that Bill was really a "good boy." I'm not saying he should have been patted on the head and told to "go and sin no more." I'm not for a moment insensible to the tragic fate of the victims whose lives he snuffed out. I'm simply pointing out that torturing the truth to picture Bill as a monster is, to me, hypocrisy.

This is the twentieth century, not the twelfth. While we have long since rejected demonology as a science, we have enthusiastically embraced it as an art. We express our outrage with horror comic books published for the young, yet on an adult level we eagerly demand the same fare. As a result, the men who report the news operate on the theory that the simple and painful truth about those who wait to die isn't good enough. It must be sensationalized, mysticized, horrorized. A certain number of monsters and fiends are essential to reportorial tradition (and circulation), which must be upheld at all cost.

Accordingly, the journalistic mythologist is always on the lookout for new candidates, examining credentials, weighing possibilities. Whenever the current crop runs low, or the public tires of being horrified and outraged by the monsters currently on display, the monster-makers invariably can be depended upon to bring forth a new one. Their skill at accomplishing this feat is so uncanny that one would be almost tempted to believe they have some sort of working arrangement with the Prince of Darkness himself. But that would be the old-fashioned approach and they are anything but old-fashioned. Actually, using only imagination and a bag of tricks, they are able to turn out a product that would make Hell blush with shame.

If clothes make the man, then words make the monster.

Once it is decided to give him the full treatment, capital is made of any physical defects, differences or deformities, however slight. If none exist, they always can be invented. Bill Cook had a drooping eyelid; so did one of England's greatest kings, but that didn't deter the papers from playing up Bill's defect as though it were the mark of monsterhood.

Because of libel laws monsters are never certified as authentic members of the genus until found guilty or insane. Yet the big buildup usually begins with the commission of the crime and continues through the trial. If there's an acquittal, the promising candidate is dropped like a hot potato. If conviction carries with it a term of imprisonment, rather than the death penalty, he fizzles out as a monster after a few days or weeks. The elements of life, death and violence are essential. The weirdest factor of all is this: if chance, fate or circumstance had acquitted or imprisoned the "monsters" presently held on the Row, and had doomed those acquitted or imprisoned, the Row still would hold the same number of monsters. The headlines would remain as big and black; the editorials denouncing them would be as muscular; the demands for their necks would be as hysterical. Only the names would be changed.

The legal niceties established, the monster is fair game. It's always open season on him. His crime or crimes are chillingly reconstructed, his imagined inhumanity is stressed. He's given a tag (red-light bandit, green-glove rapist, Manhattan maniac). Constitutionally and psychologically, he's a sinister, mysterious and alien being. He's often under the sway of lunar influences. The forces that motivate him are brutally simple: he's "kill crazy," he's "sex maddened."

Enough bad things can never be said about him. The words

used to describe him must always be scare words; they must always bristle with indignation. "Psychopath"—an epithet, not a diagnosis—is one of the best of these words; it's always proper to apply it to him and add the word "beast." It's fashionable to write to the editor of a newspaper who specializes in exposing and denouncing the monster and say, "It would be a pleasure to help exterminate [him]." It's an outrage to accord the monster due process of law.

Even the national newsmagazines are often drawn into this emotional vortex. Tacitly, subtly, they acknowledge the monster and the fiend as distinct criminal entities, thus approving and perpetuating the myth. Reading their stories is like looking into a trick mirror in a fun house.

Branding the doomed man as a monster and explaining away his crime on that basis is an evasion of social responsibility. Crime is a tough enough problem without confounding it with mythology and medieval thinking. It isn't a form of entertainment in which the audience may insist that evil must be personalized and forced to wear the trappings of a monster or a fiend, like a grotesque Halloween mask and costume, in order to heighten the emotional, essentially vengeful pleasures of the audience and deepen its prejudices. When we so symbolize and ritualize murder we dramatize not human experience but human folly.

Crime is a problem. It should be approached and dealt with as such. Murderers are men. They came to Death Row from your communities. It isn't this place that makes them different, it isn't their isolated remoteness that makes them different. Nor the scare words used to describe them, nor your fictionalized, emotionally charged opinion of them.

What makes them different is the act they committed. They took another human life. But they did not kill because they were monsters; they became monsters only because they killed and because they were tried, convicted and doomed, and the horrified public, determined to believe them *different,* was willing and eager to believe they were monsters.

Why, then, did they kill?

There is, of course, no one answer. But in each case there is an answer. In each case there were storm signals flashed, either by the man about to kill or by his environment. The law speaks vaguely, using words from the Middle Ages, of an "abandoned and malignant heart." But how and why does a "heart" (presumably the thinking and feeling essence of man) become "abandoned and malignant"? What is the source of the malignancy? Why, in the case of murder, does determinism remain merely a word in the vocabulary of the social scientist?

Which is more important, avenging murder or averting it?

Yesterday there were, today there are, and a thousand years from now there will be those blindly content to denounce the murderer as a monster and demand that he be killed off. And as long as theirs is the voice that prevails there always will be murderers to kill off. For them, objectively studying the act of murder and the complex forces and factors that produced it is morally wrong. It would amount to coddling monsters, instead of righteously damning them. Moreover, for them, such an enlightened approach would be too great an intellectual effort, too severe a social discipline. They are capable only of demanding harsher laws, of writing angry letters to editors of newspapers, of volunteering to act as executioner, of basking in their own righteousness.

They constantly profess great concern for the dead victim of a past homicide but you will never hear one word out of them for the living victim of a future homicide. You will never hear them say, "That person must be saved! How?" They would have you believe that the problem of murder (or any other serious offense) can be buried with the executed body of the perpetrator, when all that is actually buried is the solution to the problem.

That's the price *you* pay for this monstrous monster myth.

III

Only by helping the psychopath solve his problem can society expect to solve its problem of what to do about him. Solution calls not so much for concentrating on what is "wrong" with him as it does for discovering what is "right" about him.

Brain washing won't work. All attempts at "change" (that is, in psychiatric parlance, at "constructive intra-psychic reorganization")—and I don't exclude the psychoanalytic approach—have been with the explicit or implicit idea in mind that there is a "demon," metaphysical, psychopathological, instinctual or otherwise, inside the aggressive psychopath which somehow must be driven or lured out, and once that feat has been accomplished, all will be well. The notion should be discarded. In its place should be substituted a functional methodology for enabling the psychopath and his society to come to socially acceptable terms, to reach an accord satisfactory to both.

The methodology should recognize that the psychopath needs a challenge that will utilize to the fullest his drives, energies, skills; that his goal, recognized or not, is complete liberation from the wrongness within himself. It is the retention—and then the redirection—of the psychopath's distinctive identity which alone can make him whole.

Find a way to put his psychopathy to work.

The prescription produced *Cell 2455, Death Row*. It is producing this book, every word of which is being written in a Death Row cell by a man many have called hopelessly and dangerously psychopathic, a man who realizes that it may soon be his turn to enter San Quentin's lethal gas chamber. Around me violence still smolders, still bloodily erupts. Death still leers, still threatens. My neighbors continue to be marched off to the execution chamber.

The difference is that I've found myself, the hard way. I've found that it takes guts to be honest. I've found a challenge in my writing that has given my life meaning, purpose, direction. I've added a new dimension to my existence. I've learned to value love and friendship. I'm still fighting, but now it is for what I believe in. Kindness and the opportunity for self-realization have brought me willingly within the social orbit where negative, repressive measures succeeded only in fanning greater rebellion.

This is an answer to psychopathy.

IV

Your waiting is over.

Three of the executioner's assistants come for you. The cell door is unlocked, opened. You're told quietly, impersonally, "It's time."

It's time to die, to be executed.

You stand there for an instant, unmoving. Perhaps you take a last drag on your cigarette, drop the butt, step on it. Three pairs of eyes watch you.

"Go to hell!" you can scream defiantly. "I'm not going! Do you bastards hear me? I'm not going!"

They hear you. But you're going nevertheless. They'll take you by force if necessary. They have a job to do.

You can whimper. You can cry out to God to help you, to save your life. But don't expect a miracle. He won't intervene. So ask only for the strength to die like a man.

You can shrug. You didn't think it would come to this, but it did. And here you are, at the end of life's road, about to take that last short walk.

Automatically, your legs move. You're walking, mechanically—out through the death watch cell entrance, around a bend in the short hallway, through a doorway. And there it is. The gas chamber. No stopping now. No turning back. You're hustled into this squat, octagonal, glass- and metal-sided cell within a room. Its elaborate gadgets don't interest you. Quickly you find yourself seated in the No. 2 chair. The guards strap you down. Their movements are swift and sure, smoothly rehearsed. The stethoscope is connected.

There! The job is done.

"Good luck," says the guard captain in charge.

Then you're alone. The guards have left. The metal door has closed. The spoked wheel on the outside of that door is being given a final turn.

Everything is in readiness! This is the dreadful, final moment. While the physical preparations were underway, while you moved, it wasn't so real. Activity blocked full realization. It was like watching a gripping scene in a movie, where the camera had been speeded up and the action had carried you along with it, irresistibly. You had only a blurred awareness that it was leading to this. But now that you're physically immobilized, there's a jarring change. The camera slows. You see; you absorb; the scene unfolds with a terrible clarity. For an instant, time is frozen. Your thoughts and sensory impressions are fragmented, each one stabbing at you like a needle.

The warden is at his post. So is the executioner and the attending physician. On the opposite side of the chamber, behind a guard rail less than four feet from where you sit, stand the official witnesses, their eyes riveted on you through the thick glass. In a matter of minutes you'll be dead. They're here to watch *you* die.

The executioner is signaled by the warden. With scientific precision, valves are opened. Closed. Sodium cyanide eggs are dropped into the immersion pan—filled with sulphuric acid —beneath your metal chair. Instantly the poisonous hydrocyanic acid gas begins to form. Up rise the deadly fumes. The cell is filled with the odor of bitter almond and peach blossoms. It's a sickening-sweet smell.

Only seconds of consciousness remain.

.   .   .

You inhale the deadly fumes. You become giddy. You strain against the straps as the blackness closes in. You exhale, inhale again. Your head aches. There's a pain in your chest. But the ache, the pain is nothing. You're hardly aware of it. You're slipping into unconsciousness. You're dying. Your head jerks back. Only for an awful instant do you float free. Your brain has been denied oxygen. Your body fights a losing ten-minute battle against death.

You've stopped breathing. Your heart has quit beating.

You're dead.

The minutes pass. The blowers whirr. The ammonia valves are open. The gas is being driven from the cell. The clerical work is being done.

That's your body they're removing; it's your body they take to the prison morgue. No, don't worry about that cyanide rash on your leg.

If you have no one to claim your body and you're not of the Jewish or Catholic faith, you'll be shipped off to be cremated. You'll come back to the prison in a "jar." You'll go to Boot Hill.

If your body is claimed, a mortician will come for it. He'll take you away to a funeral parlor, prepare you for burial, impersonally. Services? Well, that's up to your people. Then burial. The end. But not really the end.

An aged mother may be weeping silently. She carried you in her womb. She gave you birth. And your life came to this.

"Mommy," a little girl may ask, "where's Daddy?"

Cruelly, a playmate may tell a small son, "Your old man died in the gas chamber!"

A young wife is dazed, numb.

This is your legacy to them.

· · ·

Now back to your case. You've just asked me if there isn't something I can do. Yes, there is. Your death in the gas chamber was only a horrible dream. You're not really here on Death Row at all. You're home again, free. You're sitting there reading this book about a place where men wait to die. When you reach the final page, I only hope that what I've tried to tell you has given you new insight into an age-old problem.

V

"May 2, 1960. This is being recorded at about ten fifty a.m. Caryl Chessman died about forty minutes ago . . . .

"I left the house at eight a.m., and walked out to the main gate. Reporters were gathering around with their cameras and equipment, and their cars were parked all along the street. I went down to the barricade about a quarter of a mile to the east, where the demonstrators stayed all night. One big sign read, 'This is Justice?' The people looked tired and cold. Some had obviously been there all night. Most of them were young. There was a truck selling coffee and sweetrolls.

"I walked back to the gas chamber and went in about eight twenty a.m. Father Dingberg was talking with Chessman, standing at the bars of his cell. The officers were there. I said, 'Good morning—I guess it is still a good morning.' Chessman said, 'No good news, no especially bad news.' Then he added: 'All I can say is that this is a hell of a way to start a week!'

"Chessman said he had heard the flash that the Supreme Court had gone in session about eight a.m. The radio was up, and we all waited. It was playing music; one song was 'Keep Your Sunny Side Up.' We switched stations, and the announcer said he would bring us the bulletin as soon as it came. Chessman started a last letter to his attorney, Rosalie Asher. He wrote on yellow, legal-sized paper. He crouched on the mattress or stood and bent over the metal folding shelf to write, using a pencil.

"The newscaster broke in and we all sucked in our breaths. The bulletin was that the Supreme Court had denied Caryl Chessman's petition. Further details later. This was at nine fourteen a.m. Chessman looked a long time at the clock. 'It's unfair they took so long,' he said. 'It's practically killed any chance to go further.' He looked at the clock again, and said, 'We'll have to face it. This is it.'

"At nine forty-five there were still no further details. Chess-

From the book *Death Row Chaplain* by Byron Eshelman. © 1962 by Prentice-Hall, Inc., and reprinted with permission of the author.

man said, 'Let's get packed and ready to go here.' He straightened up all the papers on his table, and told the guards, 'Well, let's get started with this white shirt routine.'

"He called Father Dingberg 'Father,' and me, 'Reverend.'

"'I appreciate knowing both of you,' he said. 'I feel a little foolish about not having a religious faith, and seeing things like you see them. In fact, I feel like a damn fool. I thought I might have a feeling now, but it's just not there. It went out of me years ago and just never came back. I don't feel I should pretend about it when it isn't there.'

"Father Dingberg said, 'Speaking for myself, I have always appreciated your straightforward attitude.'

"I told Chessman, 'Your life has left a tremendous impact on the world. Your books will be classics.'

"Chessman shook his head. 'In spite of being accused of such great ego,' he said, 'I don't believe my books will be classics, but I do hope they will have some effect on the whole problem of capital punishment.'

"Nothing was happening. Chessman paced around his cell. 'Sure I'm uneasy,' he said, 'but don't worry. I'll be able to hold up and go through with it . . . There's no use denying fear; it's just what you do with it—how you handle it—that counts.'

"He paced some more, then checked over his own body. 'I don't think I've lost any controls,' he told us. 'My ass isn't twitching, either . . . I remember one guy who came down to wait. When he came back up, the boys asked him if his ass twitched. Hell, he said, it jumped clean out of the socket.'

"Warden Dickson came in at ten to ten. Chessman asked him if he knew anything more. The warden said he'd been on the phone, but couldn't find out any more than came over the radio. Chessman gave him all the letters and documents he had written. The warden promised to take care of them.

"Chessman said he knew the warden would be asked if there were any confessions at the last minute. 'I just want to keep the record straight,' he said. 'I am not the Red Light Bandit. I am not the man. I won't belabor the point; just let it stand at that.'

"Chessman took off his shirt when the doctors came in. 'How are the adrenalins working?' a doctor asked him. Chessman said, 'I can't tell you just how they're working, Doc, but I know they're working.'

"Father Dingberg gave him a cigarette and lighted it for him. Then he shook hands with him. I shook hands with him and said, 'I'm in your corner.' He said, 'Thanks.' I wanted to say 'God bless you,' but I knew he didn't want me to.

"They waited until about one minute after ten, and then the warden gave the signal. Chessman said, 'So long, Father . . . so long, Reverend.' He walked straight past us to the gas chamber and sat down in the chair. He looked completely composed, hair combed, white shirt collar open at the neck. He smiled at the warden, and said, 'I'm all right.' Then he turned and said the same thing through the window, so that someone out there would be reassured.

"Warden Dickson nodded for the pellets to be dropped. They were. Chessman seemed to flinch each time he took a breath. There was a whispering and commotion over where the warden stood. Later I heard this was the business of the phone message from Federal Judge Goodman who was trying to stop the execution for thirty minutes to give Chessman's attorneys time to make their appeal.

"Chessman's head was back. His mouth open and his eyes closed now. When I looked in again, his head was down and saliva was dripping from his mouth.

"The witnesses filed out into the sunlight. Father Dingberg and I stood a moment by the chamber. 'I didn't think it would ever happen,' I said. He said, 'The horrible thing is what does it prove after all?'

"A minister outside stopped us and asked if either chaplain had gotten Chessman into the faith. I just told him no. One reporter asked me, 'Were you in there?' I said, 'I'm not authorized to talk to the press.'

"I could have cried. I came as close to breaking down and crying as I ever had at an execution. Walking home alone, I cried to myself. I'm crying now . . . ."

VI

Chessman's last letter to his lawyer, George T. Davis, the night before he was executed by the State of California.

Dear George:

Now my long struggle is over. Yours isn't. This barbarous senseless practice, capital punishment, will continue. In our society other men will go on taking that last walk to death until . . . when? Until the citizens of this State and this land are made aware of its futility. Until they recognize that retributive justice is no justice at all.

I die with the burning hope that my case and my death will contribute to this awareness, this realization. I know that you will personally do all in your power, as a citizen and lawyer, to convince your fellows that justice is not served, but confounded, by vengeance and executioners.

Good Luck . . . .

Clinton Duffy

Born and raised in the 'Prison Town' of San Quentin, with all but a very few of my adult years in prison work, I want to present to you the practical experience I have had for over thirty-two years in handling adult offenders, both male and female, who have been condemned to death.

I have personally witnessed over one hundred and fifty executions and have legally officiated at the execution of eighty-eight men and two women. Prior to my appointment as warden at San Quentin, I participated in sixty legal hangings.

CLINTON DUFFY began his correctional career on 1 November 1929, as secretary to the warden at San Quentin. In July 1940 he was named warden. He remained warden for eleven years until he was elevated to the adult authority (parole board). For the last several years he has lectured across the country in an attempt to abolish capital punishment. Mr. Duffy told me of the incredible strain that came with each execution he had to participate in, how he and his wife would go for long drives or sit in their car watching the ocean for hours without speaking. When I asked how he kept from going mad, he said: "But there was so much that was good occurring at the prison; there were the fifty-six hundred other men who at last were free of corporal punishment, who at last had a chance to learn, to become whole."

According to Byron Eshelman,

San Quentin is said to have derived its name from a hanging. During the early years of the nineteenth century, a sub-chief of the Licituit Indians made a modest living by stealing cattle and horses from the Spanish settlers. A posse finally trapped him near the present city of San Rafael. His name was Ken-Teen. He was reportedly hanged on a promontory jutting out into San Francisco Bay, and the site came to be known as Point Ken-Teen. Later settlers gave Ken-Teen a French spelling and called the tiny community San Quentin, a dubious honor to the northern French city of San Quentin, named in tribute to the martyred St. Gaius Quintinus.

On July 14, 1852, ... the bark *Hell Ship* anchored off Point San Quentin with fifty men and women who were prisoners of the sovereign state of California....

During its first year, the fifty-convict capacity *Hell Ship* was jammed with an additional one hundred prisoners, rounded up by sheriffs who were eager to collect their dollar-a-mile for delivering a man or woman to the prison. Living conditions were comparable to those on an African slave ship. Illness and disease were rampant, and there were no hospital facilities. Guards used clubs and straps to enforce discipline; prison breaks were attempted daily. There was not enough food for all the prisoners, but the favored few even had their own private stores of whiskey. The more attractive women were taken by the guards as their private "trustees"; the others had to fend for themselves in the filthy hold of the *Hell Ship*.

This was the progenitor of today's Death Row. The first cellblock completed by the prisoners in 1853 stood until 1959, when I watched it being razed to make room for a modern Adjustment Center building. But the conditions of the *Hell Ship* were by no means confined to the earliest days of San Quentin... Not until 1940, when Clinton Duffy became warden, were whips, straps and rubber hoses permanently banned for the punishment of prisoners.

The following is excerpted from a presentation made by Clinton Duffy at the College of the Redwoods, Fortuna, California, in mid-March, 1971.

An Evening with Clinton Duffy

Let me describe a hanging to you first; I had to participate in sixty.

When the date of the execution comes close the prisoner is taken from Condemned Row to a holding room about twenty-five feet away from the gallows. Inside this holding room is another cage where the prisoner is placed, with two mattresses on the floor, one bucket for his toilet and another for water, some reading material, if he wanted it, and writing material if he wanted to write to someone. He was under guard for twenty-four hours a day, two and sometimes three guards there, to make sure of one thing: that the commitment would be carried out and would be carried out properly; that he would not be able to commit suicide in those last few hours, or try to take someone else's life as the hours grew close, because he had nothing to lose. It was a very, very tight situation. While the men were in this holding room, most of the time they slept. Once in a while the chaplain would come up and they'd have their prayers and the like. Also the warden would visit them the night before. If they had no special requests of any kind he'd go home.

Next morning the warden went through a regular routine. First he would call the governor. If there was nothing on the governor's desk, then he would call the Court of Convictions. If they had no reason to stop the execution, he would call the state's attorney general, and if *he* had nothing on his desk to stop the execution, then the warden was ready to proceed. All this is what the law requires when the warden receives a commitment.

Then the warden proceeds to the holding cell. The chaplain of the prisoner's choice, if any, is present also. Once in a great while the prisoner says, "No, I'm an atheist; I don't want any chaplain at all—keep them away from me," and that's perfectly all right. Usually, though, the priest will be there, giving the man the last rites, or whatever his religion requires, and then everyone is ready for the execution.

The day before, the condemned has been weighed and sized. New clothes have been gotten for him, so that he can change again just prior to the execution, to make sure that there are no weapons or anything hidden. When the hour arrives and the warden gives him the sign, the executioner goes in and straps the man's hands to his side. Prior to that, of course, the warden has had a few words with the man. Then the warden gives another nod and two guards go in. One takes the man by one elbow and one by the other, and they lead him from this holding cell through the door, up the thirteen steps, and place him on the gallows platform trap door. After that the procedure goes very quickly, like clockwork.

Just to the right on the gallows platform there's a little room with walls about seven feet high. Three men, usually guards, are seated there on stools. In front of them there is a shelf and across this shelf there are very taut strings, one in front of each man. One of those strings springs the trap that causes the execution. Two of them drop to the floor below, connected to buckets of sawdust—the equivalent of blanks in a gun. Each man has a very sharp shoemaker's knife in his hand, waiting for a signal.

The condemned man is placed on the gallows platform trap door and another guard straps his ankles together. Then the executioner takes the noose from the cross rod above, puts it over the man's head, and cinches it up behind the left ear. There is a black cap that goes over his head, too, to keep you, the witnesses, from seeing the gruesome effect at the end of the rope after the trap has been sprung. Then the executioner raises his hand, at the nod of the warden, and the men in this little room pull their knives across these very taut strings. The trap springs. Witnesses pass out or become sick; many of them have to be carried or led from the witness room; it's quite gruesome. A doctor gets on a stool, in front of the man; he rips open his white shirt and with a stethoscope listens to the heartbeat. It takes between eight and fifteen minutes, according to the vitality of the individual, before the heart stops. That's the legal time of death.

Then the warden dismisses the witnesses. They all sign the register and go out. But the warden allows the body to remain at the end of the rope for another ten, fifteen minutes at his will. Again, the reason is that the commitment says: "you shall be hanged by the neck until you are dead." And the warden wants to make sure that the order of the commitment has been carried out. Finally, when the warden gives the order, they cut the body down and put it in a casket, a redwood box. Then the executioner cuts the noose from around the man's neck and takes off the black cap. And there you see that the side of the face has been torn open in more cases than not, and the whole face is disfigured; it's very gruesome. As I said, sometimes the neck has been broken and sometimes the man has strangled to death. But that is not important as far as the execution is concerned.

I've never seen an electrocution, but I've been told by other wardens it's an equally gruesome affair. At San Quentin, however, we had lethal gas executions, and of my eighty-eight men and two women all but one were executed by lethal gas. If there can be any such thing as a humane way to perform an execution, it might be lethal gas. But if you can call lethal gas humane, it's only in one way: the loved ones taking the body home for burial do not have a disfigured body, as they do in hanging or the electrical chair.

I don't think that capital punishment is the deterrent that it's supposed to be at all. We will never know that. But we might look at a couple of examples.

We used to receive, and still do receive in our state prisons today, a great number of commitments from Los Angeles

County. It's the largest county in the state. Many people come from other states into the Los Angeles area: glamorous Hollywood, Disneyland, all of those places. Sometimes they go broke and they commit crimes. One deputy sheriff there brought prisoners to me every week or so—sometimes a whole train load, as many as a hundred, two hundred, in one shipment. And when he'd deliver his men he'd come over and we would have a chat. We'd talk about politics. We'd talk about sports, or the weather. We'd talk about crime—about the death penalty. He brought men to be executed. He brought thieves, forgers, sex offenders, you name it; they all came under his direction, as a deputy sheriff. He booked them in by the hundreds under every section of the Penal Code you can think of, including murder and other crimes for which men are condemned to death.

He killed his wife. And when he came to San Quentin to be executed, I went to the Row on the third day after his arrival and I said to this man, "Al, how come you didn't think of the death penalty? You've brought men to me for years." And he said, "Look, I planned the murder of that woman. I wanted to get rid of her. There was no other way in my mind except to kill her, and I did it very, very seriously, with precision, and when I finished the job I realized right after that I had committed a wrong. I had not at one time thought of the death penalty prior to the commission of this act. I should have. There was another way out. I could have handled it differently. But I killed her —and I'm sorry—but it's too late now. I did not think of the death penalty."

We changed over from hanging to lethal gas in the mid-thirties. And we had a young man in San Quentin that was a thief. He stole from department stores. He was a pretty good thief: he made a living of it, except, of course, when he got caught and came to prison. At that time we needed some men to build the lethal gas chamber, to work as laborers: mixing cement, threading pipe and the like. And so this young fellow was assigned. He was a hunchback, kind of a likeable guy, and every night when he'd come back into the Big Yard he'd be surrounded by the men. Many of them would say to him, "Tell us about the lethal gas chamber; tell us about the torture chamber." And he'd give them a blow-by-blow description of the progress of installation. Invariably he would say, "Fellas, this is as close as I ever want to get to the gas chamber."

He was in for about three and a half, four years; then he went out. He had been out maybe three and a half years in the free world when he killed two of his relatives and a friend. He was enamoured of a half-sister; they tried to break it up, and he killed these people that were bothering him.

He came to be executed. And I asked him what I asked the deputy sheriff. He gave me a similar answer, only in different words: "When the devil gets into you, you think of nothing else."

Shouldn't the man who was a deputy sheriff and the man who helped install the gas chamber have thought of the death penalty? I think they should have.

Capital punishment is not equal in its application, as we all know. I could take you into San Quentin, to Folsom, Sing Sing, Joilette, anywhere where they might have the death penalty, and I could give you, ten-to-one, men whose cases in the Big Yard are just as bad, if not worse, than some of those on Condemned Row.

Three men had been following the crops in California. They ran out of work in Fresno and were going on to Bakersfield, riding the rails. The three ran out of the canned heat and cheap wine they had been drinking. They saw another man at the other end of the boxcar reach in his pocket, pull out a dirty old dollar bill, look at it and put it back in his pocket. He was drunk too. At the next stop they asked him to get off and buy a cheap bottle of wine. He refused. The next stop they asked him again. And he refused with a few cuss words. At the third stop they asked him once again, a little more violently. And he got more violent in his cussing and his response. So they stomped him. And they stomped him to death. Two of them were sentenced by the judge—they didn't ask for a jury trial—to be executed. The third received a life sentence. And this is part of the record; the judge said to this third man: 'I am giving you a life sentence because you put a band-aid on the finger of a bystander in the box. You will get life—the other two shall be executed."

Let's compare that to the case of two other men, farmers, who had been fighting and feuding over property rights in one of the northeastern counties of California. They must have been feuding for quite some time, and finally one of them couldn't stand it any longer. He saw his neighbor going to town that morning so he parked his jeep sideways across an access road going into their properties from the highway. And he waited about seventy feet away behind some bushes with a fully loaded 30-30 rifle, for three hours. When his neighbor finally came back and couldn't get by the jeep parked across the road he got out of his car and said, "What's going on here?" and this fellow pumped five 30-30 slugs into him. Second degree murder. Five years to life. Twenty-one months—not years—twenty-one months minimum term. If that wasn't pre-meditation, three hours lying in wait, I don't know what pre-meditation means. Versus a drunken brawl and executed. And you can find all kinds of similar cases throughout the whole United States.

I'm going to ask you whether or not you've ever known of a wealthy person to have been executed in the history of the United States. I call execution a "privilege of the poor." Now please don't say to yourself that wealthy people do not kill. Yes, they do. We have them in the state of California serving time right now, for murder, where the district attorney tried his best, in individual cases in separate counties, to get the death penalty. It was impossible. Nothing wrong with the trial; as honest as could be. But an attorney well versed in the handling of such cases is employed by the defendant. They go on and on with the trial and it just takes forever. The attor-ney's well paid. He knows all the tricks. This versus a man who defends someone who doesn't have any money; he gets a pit-tance from the state and has other things he has to do: run his office, support his home.

It is documented that innocent people have been executed in America. The state of Maine abolished the death penalty because they hanged a man who was later proved to be innocent. And that's been true in other incidents as well. It's too late. You cannot bring those men back. That's just one of the reasons why we should abolish the death penalty, among others.

Here is a story for those who may believe in capital punishment. It began when I was a young man growing up in a prison town. There was a man and his wife who used to come to San Quentin with their son, to visit their aunt and uncle who also had a boy my age. The three of us became buddies, a threesome. He used to come on the weekends when the executions were on Friday. And he would argue with me: "Get rid of these beasts. They're no good. Drown them all. Hang 'em. Shoot 'em. Get them out of our hair. No need of keeping them in these penitentiaries. Kill 'em all." And I would say, "No, it's wrong to kill." And as we grew up, we argued. He married; he was a little bit older. A boy was born. I used to play with the youngster. I used to ride him around San Quentin on my bicycle.

He grew up. He killed a merchant in San Francisco. He was sentenced to be executed. I was the warden. And this man who had been so adamant about capital punishment—a professional man—came and told me, "Clint, you have to help me save my boy. I used to say 'get rid of all these beasts; they're no good.' Here my boy is going to be executed. The only child we have—our own flesh and blood. You have to help me save him."

I had to lead that boy into the gas chamber. The man, within four or five months, died of a broken heart and alcoholism. Why didn't he stay with his belief in capital punishment for his own child? It was good enough for somebody else, but not good enough for him.

Some states have abolished the death penalty recently. New York abolished the death penalty with the exception of peace officers and prison personnel killed in the line of duty. New York in 1965; then Vermont, West Virginia, Iowa, Oregon.

The latest was in 1969—New Mexico. The whole common-wealth of England has abolished the death penalty completely in the last two or three years.

Executions are going out gradually by disuse. In 1935 there were almost two hundred in the United States. In 1952, eighty-three. In '64, forty-seven. In '64, fifteen. In '65, seven. In '66, one. In '67, two. In '68, '69, '70 and now '71—none. There are thirteen states that have abolished the death sentence com-pletely.

This question comes to me regularly: "If we abolish the death penalty in California"—or wherever we might be—"our whole state's going to go down the drain. More crime, more murder, more homicides." Have you ever heard of the state of Michigan going down the drain? *1847*—not 19—*1847*. They abolished the death penalty completely and do you know that in the state of Michigan, where it's been abolished, there are fewer homicides than in the capital punishment state of Illi-nois, the next-door neighbor. There are more homicides per hundred thousand in the state of Illinois with the death pen-alty than there are in the state of Michigan without the death penalty. There are more homicides in the state of Washington with the death penalty than there are in the neighboring state of Oregon without the death penalty.

Times have changed. They don't drown people at sea any longer. They don't dissect your body bit by bit because you committed some crime. They don't hang you in public like they used to in England because you were a pickpocket. Those things are not being done any longer. But we do have the elec-tric chair. We do have the gallows. We do have the lethal gas chamber, the firing squad. And I think that if we do away with all these we're all going to be the better for it.

Dovie C. Mathis

Dovie Carl Mathis, A-84403, Death Row, San Quentin, California, is "inside editor" for a portion of this book. His strength and personal conviction have created the kind of trust on the Row which allowed him to select and edit the works of Josh Hill and Doc Varnum appearing in these pages. Another introduction of Dovie's opened up the communication which led to the inclusion of Dan Roberts's material. This book would not have been the same without Dovie's considerable help.

Perhaps his strength comes from the fact that he is fighting for his life against incredible odds. He sincerely claims innocence of a murder for which he was convicted: a killing in a lover's triangle which a dissenting judge once stated was at most a second degree murder and not at all an executable act. Twice since 1964 he has gone back to court for a new penalty hearing on his case. Twice he has been sentenced to death.

As you know, Stephen, both the original and recent transcripts of my trial and retrial contain a love letter which Alice wrote me, offering me money, expressing her love for me, which she denied under oath in court. The D.A.'s case in chief against me was based on perjured testimony. I was proclaimed the liar, but in fact, was the only one who testified to the actual truth. Billy Still has filed writs in every state and federal court admitting that his testimony was *perjured* and *untrue!* I can get statements from other witnesses who knew Alice was in love with me—and when I finally rejected her, that's when her and Still set their mad notion into actions which resulted in the death of her husband—and me being convicted, condemned and sent to DEATH ROW....

Dovie's life, like the lives of the others in this book, is an incredible complex of irony and mishap. He received his first date of execution on the same day that he was served with divorce papers from his wife of over ten years. Twice his life has been saved from the executioner by writs from Dan Roberts, whose work follows later in this book. His fight is for justice even more than for life.

Seven years ago, when first arriving at Death Row, he wrote his parents, "I met some fellows here who got many books on law and those books tell you how the law works. Well, this one guy said he would teach me about it, and I do want to learn many things to better me, better my education, and then maybe I can write a book some day." His book *From Symbol to Spear, to Fashion of Fist* will be published next year.

It is our hope that someday we might "sit by a stream and watch our children play together."

As he once wrote:

> Let America have her treasures
> And rejoice over her ephemeral pleasures,
> For I, Immortal Man, have no ending.

Life's Hidden Season

Dovie C. Mathis

30 May 1964

Dear Mother and Father:

I'm sure by now Sylvia and Rezell have told you about the bad news, about I was sentenced to die in the "gas chamber." I know how much hurt you both must feel about it, and me trying to tell you how I feel will just hurt you some more, but I know I have to say something sometime.

I got sentenced yesterday, May 29, and Sylvia and Rezell were in court that morning. Sylvia she couldn't help but to cry, but Rezell she didn't; she did a little bit better about it. They let us have a visit when I got back over to the jail. I tried to joke about it to make them feel better but they don't. Sylvia she still cry some more, but me, I don't give a damn, the witnesses they lied for the police and district attorney to help frame me, the judge wouldn't let in any of the evidence to prove I was innocent, and my attorney didn't call one witness to testify for me. I asked him why and he said he couldn't. I had no defense for myself, and might as well have had no lawyer.

The police were a bunch of dirty lying dogs, they called me nigger and kept saying I was lying to them when I'd try to tell them what really happened that night. They kept saying they were going to send me to "DEATH ROW," even when I kept telling them that Ray jumped on me with a tire iron and I ran to keep from fighting with him. But when he caught me and jumped on me again I fought him back, but I didn't kill him.

39

Even if I killed him it wasn't no murder, but I didn't kill him, but who cares but the family.

I met some fellows here who got many books on law and those books tell you how the law works. Well, this one guy said he would teach me about it, and I do want to learn about many things to better me, better my education, and then maybe I can write a book some day. I'm gonna study hard and in a few years I will be like a new man. I just got some of those books. They are big and the words are long, big and hard to understand, but I'll learn, I'll learn. I am sorry how I hurt you, but please don't hate me. I can make it only if you go on loving me as I will always love you both. Take care of yourselves for me.

Your son,
Dovie C. Mathis

As time passed, Dovie's growth was manifested on several levels. Brother Wilson of the Church of Christ devoted much time to him. "He was perceptive enough to see beyond the surface. Because of him my thoughts, my way of thinking has changed—a thorough and total rebirth. ..."

22 September 1965

My Dear Brother Wilson:

It was an honor to see you again, and to be joined with you in prayer, being worthy of your valuable time and wonderful teaching. I too share great pleasure when I find myself in the presence of such a devoted man, wise counselor and beloved brother. And truly, my brother, it has been a most wonderful, enlightening—rare experience to know you. I regret it was ordained that we meet under such unfortunate circumstances; but nevertheless, it is an occasion, an experience that I shall always hold with my highest and deepest thoughts and feelings.

Although I was brought up in a Christian family, because of many bad experiences with those who proclaimed themselves teachers or preachers, before you began teaching me several months ago—I had lost all my confidence in Christianity—not actually Christianity itself, but the misleading way in which it was being taught, by some hypocrites who preached the saving of souls while they themselves were devoted and dedicated to committing evils and sins; preaching of goodness, rightness and a sense of spiritual values with their voice, while their minds snaked through poor people's pockets. But you have been teaching me Christianity in a way I had never heard it taught before. I weigh your teaching on the scales of my own logic and reason and find that we are more and more becoming in tune and harmony with the songs of God's religious symphony. However, as I have stated from the beginning—before I submit or commit myself to God's plan of salvation for the saving of my soul, it must be based upon my own belief, my decision; not because of your belief or decision, nor because it is what you feel is best for me. For if or when I make that transition from sinner to Christian I shall place all my powers to bear on being among the best.

8 January 1966

Dear Mary:

I continue to hope and pray that these thoughts and words shall discover you and our dear daughters well and maintaining in every respect. This is my third attempt to get through to you—meaning that since I have been here on Death Row I have written two previous communications to you, but my attempts have been to no avail. I have been scheduled to die 1 March 1966, so I thought I would give it a last try—since I have so much to say, and so little time left to say it.

After years of silence between us, considering my present predicament, the words I shall try to piece together will be far from easy; but I shall humble myself; I shall hope, even beg that you will bear with me—grant me the benefit of your best understanding. Your understanding is the one thing I am totally unworthy of—yet, I seek it.

I shall not even attempt to try and expound the many "whys" —because the word *why* has plagued mankind since the beginning of time. And, too, it would take a complete novel to express and explain all the things and thoughts which have stampeded through my mind, what my heart feels and desires to say to you since our separation; but as vague and unimportant as this may seem at this precarious point, I have spent many millions of moments thinking of you, Jacqueline, and Denise—our beautiful daughters. I have spent more time in those thoughts than I can recall. I have attempted to write you what seems like a thousand times, but while my heart kept saying yes, my mind kept telling me—no! You gave me my chance, many chances, but I could not come through for you, so why interfere with your life, your new future and prospect of happiness now? I could find no pleasure or consolation in such an act, only cruelty.

I have been informed that you feel I hate you for the testimony you gave against me at my trial. Please be perfectly assured, I feel quite the contrary about you. Is it so surprising, or perhaps strange, to admit that I yet love you? Sometimes in the midst of deep and close contemplation I have come to realize how very much I did love you. I loved you with a love that was more than love. It was a powerful and profound passion which went to the heart of veneration. We shared an eccentric, but rare (love) relationship: a relationship that destiny, or immaturity (call it what you will), denied us; a relationship that I have longed, that I have willed, to grasp once more in life—to hold and cherish the many splended things love holds between man and woman, husband and wife: love which really does make the world go around and gives greater purpose and meaning to our existence.

Pride or dignity in a just or righteous cause, in pursuit of justice over injustice, is the mark of great nobility; but pride has no season in pursuit of love, understanding, peace and happiness. False and stubborn pride is the burden-bearer, the guilty slayer of many could-have-been-beautiful loves, relationships and friendships, which otherwise could have been everlasting. I have never regretted the things we did when we were together, only the things we did not do. But I have regretted most our misguided passion, our inability to try and understand each other, our misplaced sense of values, our love which we selfishly permitted to wither and die in the sun of neglect; but above all, I regret we permitted our ignorance and indifferences, differences and hang-ups to deprive our innocent children of their right to both their mother and father. I cannot rationalize it for my own self-comfort, because there is no justification. I regret fate found it fit to bring us together—and has since succeeded at tearing us apart, keeping us apart.

What can I say of significance save ask your forgiveness for the hurt and moments of misery I have caused you and our children? I am sure since last I saw them they have grown like wild grass! Perhaps I have lost the right to call them my children, but that is a part of nature we cannot change. It's a fact. I have short-changed you and them badly, but by doing so, I have short-changed myself even more. I would gladly and willingly pay any price to change the course of our past but I cannot. You know, Mary, it is amazing how very clear we can see ourself, our faults and folly when we are looking back.

I suppose I have said all that can be said at this time, except I will you love, peace and the richness of happiness in the future. I hope you shall write me tomorrow or, at least, soon, so I can live again before I die.

Much of the love I am sending is to be given to our lovely young ladies. The fact the district attorney coerced you into giving false testimony against me is absolutely no basis for hating you—nor him for that matter. If it be a consolation to you—you are forgiven. Forget it. May you continue to have the blessings and guidance of God. . . .

Church of Christ
1215 LAUREL AVENUE
EAST PALO ALTO, CALIFORNIA
322-0053

To whom it may concern:

I, Grover C. Wilson, minister of the Church of Christ, visited Bill Steel in the San Jose jail. During this visit, Mr. Steel stated that Carl Mathis, who was accused of robbery and murder, did not rob the man, but he, Bill Steel, did take the man's wallet from his pocket while Carl Mathis and the man were fighting. I asked Mr. Steel why did he involve Mr. Mathis in the robbery, and he stated that after hearing the statements that Mr. Mathis made on tape, he thought that these statements would make things worse for him; therefore, he had to say that Mr. Mathis was in on the robbery too. He also said that Mr. Mathis did not get any of the money.

Mr. Steel also stated that Mr. Mathis fought with the man and struck him one time with a rock, but neither he nor Mr. Mathis killed the man. He also stated that there was a white car parked near the place where the fighting took place.

MINISTER, GROVER C. WILSON

Subcribed and sworn to before this 27th Day of December...1965
Donald L. Brown
Notary Public – California
County Of Santa Clara

24 January 1966

My dear brother Wilson:

Thank you for the affidavits, for the call you made to my ex-attorney on my behalf, and for your thoughtful words of wisdom and encouragement. As you know, my execution is presently scheduled for 1 March 1966. The attorney who handled my trial and appeal to the state supreme court abandoned my case without giving me the benefit of notification or immediately forwarding my trial transcripts to me; therefore, in my recent petition to the state supreme court *in forma pauperis,* all I had to go on were the briefs he had initially filed and my memory—which was inconsiderate and incompetent of him knowing the critical condition such needless negligence would leave me in, indicative of the concern and enthusiasm he has shown toward me and my case from the very beginning, and typical of most of the attorneys of the men under a sentence of death, who would have never made it to the brink of disaster had they had the protection of competent counsel at trial.

I am copying this attorney's recent letter since it is the perfect portrait of how some attorneys relate themselves with regard to condemned men.

Dear Mr. Mathis,

I understand that you filed a petition with the supreme court of the state in which you referred to me as an incompetent. That is probably true, but I sort of resent people pointing it out.

I suggest to you that you are filing the wrong writs in the wrong courts and that you get on with all haste with the preparation of a petition of *certiorari* in the Supreme Court of the United States. (That is a different court than the Supreme Court of the State of California.) I understand that this court has granted *certiorari* in about five cases arising under the *Escobedo* case and that it is granting indefinite stays in all other cases until those five can be decided and some further guidelines laid down.

I want you to understand that I am not terribly concerned about what happens to you one way or the other, but I do think it is shameful that a defendant in your position cannot have high quality legal representation.

My Brother, for the black man, poor, and other less fortunate, that's how the wheel of so-called justice spins. But please be perfectly assured that I shall put forth all the knowledge and legal wisdom I have taught myself during the seventeen months I have been here on Death Row to bear upon executing a legal endeavor that shall bear the fruit of success. I am confident I shall prevail—and with the wisdom and divine guidance of God—I cannot fail.

COME IN DEATH

Death, I hear your approaching steps down the hall,
But your noise and laughter don't perturb me at all.
We've barely missed meetings—many times before;
This may surprise you, but I deem you not as my foe!
No, Death! I fear you not,
For you'll deliver me from a hell of a spot.

You shan't descend upon me as you have on billions before,
I knew how you'd be arriving—several years ago!
I was ever fascinated by your name;
That's why I challenged you with various games!
It's the weak and cowards whom you terrorize and intimidate,
When in reality—you're an unescapable fate.

O yes! You're shrewd and devious, by assorted ways you come;
And I'll even concede, you're a stealthy son-of-a-gun!
Each moment edges you nearer and nearer to me;
But I smile from the reflection of peace that I shall soon see!
Good and joyful times I've had, and thrills and bliss galore,
No! You shall never cheat me, Death—I have lived before.

You convey an air of mystery; but a stranger? No!
For long is the procession of others you've chosen to go:
Race, creed nor color hold you back,
For the red and yellow you take, as well as the white and black!
No—prejudice you're not, that I know,
You take the exceedingly rich and the extremely poor.

Impartial . . . You are! I respect your honesty and truth,
You take the young, the faded and new,
And the good and bad in no indifferent way;
So come in, Death,—I'm rejoiced to make the journey;
It's such a beautiful day . . . .

12 December 1966
Two days before set execution of 14 December 1966
Stayed for the second time at the last moment with the aid of a writ
by fellow inmate Dan Roberts.

My Beloved Mary,

Jacqueline had written me a letter with regard to your pending marriage plans for December. I had hoped it was not true, but I was inclined to believe it was true; or rather I was afraid you would one day come to tell me it was true. I had concluded from your space of silence something was wrong—or about to happen. But whether we like it or not life itself is a war; love (for us) was a war we have been fighting for so long, since we met and married in the autumn of 1954. Yes, love was the war we were fighting and death is a part of war—if the two opposing forces or parties do not come to terms with a peace treaty. But being I was neither a good example nor husband when I was free and we were together—I have no avenue for escape at the present but to feel the pain and regret from a feeling of an irreplaceable loss. Although I will that your life, your future be crowned with the jewels of happiness, I must admit your marriage destroyed all my bases for hope, which I held dearer and nearer than I thought. I read and re-read your letter. After that I was embraced with horrible emptiness and a heavy burden of loneliness. Although I realize now that, in truth, since your return I have not had you as my own, the hope of having you as my own never left me even though from time to time you would take your body away, meaning: you stopped writing, you stopped coming to see me. But I felt the full impact of that sense of loss the other day when I discovered the bases for my hope had been destroyed. As long as we have hope we have a healthy companion. With a touch of selfishness I give you up— seeing and hoping there is a possibility of you being happy and contented with someone else.

I think you are wrong for assuming you are responsible for the pain and troubles I have encountered. The truth is you were just the door-woman; I made the choice to come into love, pain and misfortune. Life is only as sweet or bitter as we make it. I believe that—and accept my own. We both were imperfect, possessing areas of immaturity as every human being does. Nevertheless, I think I gave you (since the new me) a just and honest appraisal of your "dids, didn'ts and deeds" with me. You inspired my mind and heart to seek and find some of the most beautiful pearls of wisdom and understanding my mind and heart had ever conceived, and since your return I have not shown myself ungrateful, but the contrary. So being that we both were incomplete in our love and belief in each other, it was inevitable our (love) interest would result in incompleteness, from our incompleteness. Considering my circumstances I was not open to receive or seize my new chance to correct my mistakes of the past with you. May all the forces of good unite to help you secure the completion you seek elsewhere.

Since you cannot make me be both, which will it be: I the Villain or I the Victim? This is my concession, my confession, my creed.

Go, my Love, my Life, and stay in peace . . . .

THE HOUSE OF FOOLS

A frigid retreat by the Bay—filled with men,
Some not really bad, others decayed from sin!
Behind those huge grey walls you dream—even cry;
Some await another chance to live; others wait to die.

The cliffs are bare, dull and cold,
The men within are hostile and bold!
Where little can you lean or depend upon,
For your elusive days of freedom—have flown.

Your deepest secrets are no more to be,
For your indwelling is on display, for all to see;
It assassinates your pride and wounded mentality,
And twists your vision, to Life's Realities.

Here, where dreams are more precious than gold,
Here, where you contemplate times of old;
Waiting for fate to remove the dirt,
Hoping that time will seal the hurt.

Each dawn you must endure, with dignity and shame,
But can we say that we, and we alone, are to blame?
Living in a sphere of feeble rationalization,
Confronted daily—by the greatest temptations.

Some say hell arrives after judgment day,
But I say hell is a pastel city, sitting by the Bay!
Here, you hurt, you suffer in every substance pore,
Men become more bitter tomorrow, than the day before.

The souls who sit in condemnation, eager to impress,
With lean regards—if any, of what would be best.
Justice is then so pure, it sits there and drools,
Punish, punish, punish it says: cast him away in
The House of Fools . . . .

In December 1970 Blanche Bontempi introduced me to Dovie. While working together he told me of their meeting:

Brother Stephen:

Blanche and I met in mid-April 1970 in the visitation room at the Santa Clara County jail in San Jose, California, where I was being retried on the penalty phase of my case. I had been visiting briefly with my younger sister Sylvia, who had to leave immediately because of our father's sudden and unexpected illness. I was left sitting there alone in a little isolated booth—pondering my father's fate, scanning over the lovely female scenery sitting and standing there around me, digging on the diversity of poses they displayed, their charming smiles and touching tears, their laughter.

Across from me Blanche was seated talking to a handsome young man who I later learned was her son. Several minutes passed; she stood up, paused, then moved to one of the stools stationed in front of my isolated cage, picked up the telephone, and politely asked: "Are you waiting for someone?" I smiled softly and replied, "No." She continued, "Do you mind if I talk with you?" "Quite the contrary," I assured her.

In as few words as possible I attempted to explain why I happened to be sitting there alone . . . my return from Death Row and some of my experiences during my five-year stay there . . . and the status of my present legal position, which seemed to interest her intensely. There was curiosity, concern and compassion in her voice, and in the questions she asked. After complimenting me on my courageousness, my seeming lack of fear in spite of the seriousness of my situation, she said: "With your writing, drawing and legal works and all—I don't suppose you have much time for writing letters . . . I'd like to write you." I assured her it would not be an imposition.

Moments before my time expired we exchanged names. Our farewell that special evening was punctuated with her promise: "I shall write." Two weeks hence our correspondence began. We have had a close contact and communication since. Thus far it has all been golden and good . . . .

Dear Blanche:

Regarding my appeal: it is still pending before the United States Supreme Court. However, the Court recesses in June and does not convene until mid-autumn; therefore, I do not anticipate their decision before the spring of 1971. In the meantime, I am presently on trial on the penalty phase of my conviction, which only determines the degree of penalty—Life or Death. The People presented their case this week and it should be completed in its entirety Monday evening. It should take the remainder of the week—or perhaps more—to present my defense. Since one cannot conjecture what a jury might decide . . . I shall just say, I remain hopeful. But whatever my rendezvous with destiny awards me, I shall not be left beat nor bitter. I am prepared to face it, but I shall never accept it, nor permit my spirit to be destroyed or my soul crushed by the heavy boulder of this flagrant injustice . . . .

> In silent flight
> Our souls take wings,
> And sometimes touch
> The Edge of Things;
> And our desires
> Become our Destiny.

Dear Blanche:

I regret having to tell you the action I have been involved in here in recent weeks—the verdict went against me. The judge was totally partial toward the People. Nevertheless, the adverse verdict did not sever the ever soaring wings of my spirit . . . . It was just another among a long procession of setbacks and disappointments I have had to overcome in my pursuit of truth and justice. As you know, battles are won on the same fields on which they are lost! And too, this has not affected the status of my appeal presently pending before the United States Supreme Court. I also plan to appeal this verdict, and I am confident it will be reversed by the state supreme court.

Things are never as bad as they seem or sound . . . only to the degree (or extent) we permit them to affect us . . . In another eight to eighteen months I shall return, at which time I shall make that giant step from condemned to freedom . . . .

Being innocent of the crime of which I stand convicted and condemned makes my critical situation more comfortable to bear, a little less embarrassing. Still, I would not exchange my suffering and pains of yesterday for all the joys of tomorrow. For each pain was a step that brought me closer to a higher plane in my quest for knowledge and wisdom, truth and understanding. Today, my thoughts and mental stability are anchored in life's depth: I seek the profound and permanent; I seek quality not quantity; and I seek happiness now by limiting my desires, rather than making desperate attempts to satisfy them. I strive to be pragmatic. Happiness emanates from within—not without . . . .

5 August 1970

Beloved Blanche:

I watched that program "Inside San Quentin." It was somewhat exaggerated, but it was also enlightening to those who are not aware of prison life and the conditions under which humans are compelled to live. However, everything in creation has an opposite. Every evil has its possible good . . . every positive has its opposite negative. There is a profound truth in Johnny Cash's songs and philosophy. It is so difficult to get the public interested in prisons, and the papers are reluctant to discuss the problem; it is as if they hope to remove, to delete, the entire prison picture from the national consciousness as though it was a national trauma; something to be exorcised rather than to be understood. It seems they are looking for scapegoats rather than solutions—a hopeless revenge upon the irrevocable past. Prisons fail to do what they were designed to do, and to be punitive without a point corrupts rather than chastens. Nevertheless, if one is impelled to be imprisoned, he should not just serve time . . . but let time serve him.

Condemned Row has the elite of prison comforts: permanently positioned TVs, operative from each cell, and dual-channel radios which change each hour to cover all variations of music; each cell block has a stereophonic record machine, and we are permitted to buy or have sent in any records we desire; one-man cells are bearable (it is up to each individual how clean he wishes to keep it; I am a bug for neatness); they don't furnish typewriters, but most men have their own; we have access to law books and other reading materials such as books and newspapers; etc., etc. I have my own personal and legal library which is very efficient; and the canteen is satisfactory. Visits take place in one of the two isolated rooms reserved for Condemned Row, with physical contact being permissible. I get along well with the staff who are usually more pleasant than not.

Our recreation time is limited to the long light and breezy corridor atop the north block, with various equipment for exercise, amusement and entertainment: an assortment of games such as chess, cards and dominoes; weights, ping-pong and punching bags; library, TVs and record player, etc. For the coffee connoisseurs, it's served every thirty minutes. Breakfast is served between eight and eight thirty a.m.; thereafter, I prepare for the exercise period which runs from ten thirty to two o'clock p.m. Some mornings I rest in, sleep in, but usually I come out and spend the time discussing law and other subjects with my good friend Thomas L. Varnum, whom I have known since my first day here (he has a brilliant mind and has also been and remains a devoted friend). On occasions we walk, work out on the bags, or perhaps just sit around and spin record albums from our "vast collection." Dinner is served between two and two thirty (the quality is acceptable); afterwards, I sleep or just relax until six p.m.—then into the evening light I write, answer personal letters, read and study law, or watch a few TV programs or a movie providing it appears appealing. I am usually in bed, retired for the night, an hour or so past midnight.

Unfortunately, I have not participated in any of the "art

shows"—not because of a lack of desire, but because of a lack of such privilege. Condemned Row is prohibited from the sale of any art or literary works which can be construed as manuscript materials.*

To those who are confined or imprisoned in any institution, mail is the one medication that helps heal . . . .

You ask me why love and friendship are such critical matters with me. It is a long story so I shall attempt to keep it short, but hopefully comprehensible:

Being notoriously loyal has placed me in many vulnerable situations to stop arrows with my back—fired from the bows of betrayals of past loves and friends. It was my alleged best friend who teamed up with the People of California against me, and in essence it was his false implications and confession which convicted me. He later retracted his testimony, but by then the damage had been done, and my destiny hinged upon a question of law—rather than facts! It was an insidious evil. The criterion of cruelty or evilness is not the act itself, but rather the motive behind it. I later learned the source of his motive: jealousy and envy. Billy (my best friend) built the gallows . . . Mary (my ex-wife), whom I loved better than life itself, supplied the noose. I do not use those incidents as a measuring stick to judge the integrity and sincerity of others, but as a reminder to be cautious in similar situations. I prefer to run with the prey rather than stalk with the hunter!

---

* Because of this prohibition Associate Warden Park would not allow Mathis to draw on the letters he sent. This, he was told, was to prevent him from selling any art work on the outside. He was restricted only to the drawing of flowers, which eventually he was able to imbue with human characteristics. Because Mathis had been a professional cartoonist before being committed to Death Row, Park once told him that he was watched more closely than anyone else on the Row lest he try to "sneak" any art to the outside.

THE EXECUTION OF AARON MITCHELL

'Twas a little past one in the afternoon,
The day was flying by much too soon;
Suddenly, the silence was broken by a loud cry,
From one of the condemned who was doomed to die.

There were no further appeals he could foresee,
So he begged, he pleaded—"Lord—Please save me!"
His screams and cries shattered the still day;
"I'm coming Lord, help me Jesus," was all he did say.

He began slashing himself just below the elbow;
The tears ran, the praying echoed, the blood flowed!
Only God knew what he felt inside—could not hide.
Whatever he felt, overruled his dignity and his pride.

The human had suffered in this sanctuary of hell,
A hell known to many other men as well.
He faced a fate many fear and dread,
Yet it's hard to understand what made him so afraid.

I listen to the final clinking of the chains,
Asking myself: "Is that man really sane?"
He fell apart, that much we all assumed;
Still, I shall never forget—that horror in the afternoon.

The news of his destruction (murder) spread fast,
The peace we'd known had ended at last!
But should we elude reality—permit her to stray,
And justice escape us, we shall experience that horror
By other men—another day . . . .

*Composed on the afternoon preceding Aaron Mitchell's execution
12 April 1967.*

After a few letters it was apparent that Dovie was able and willing to aid in the compilation of this book. He had had a similar idea nearly a year before: "Reflections of the Condemned," thirty-four pages of writings by ten condemned men, composed for a college teacher to assist her in a class.

While contacting other men Dovie tried on several occasions to get "Reflections" out to me, but it was blocked by prison authorities and returned again and again to its sender. As I wrote to a friend about getting materials approved and out of the prison: "It is a slow winter river returning salmon to the sea." Dovie's communication offered the first insights into the writer's condition on Death Row.

Brother Stephen:

It was a deep disappointment to me having "Reflections" returned after more than two weeks, insomuch as, more than hoping—I was confident it was in your possession and you'd had the opportunity to read it. Besides being explicit as to the purpose of it being sent to you, and that it was to be returned to me when you had completed your examination, I was asked to send down, and did send down, a D-2505: PERCENTAGE TO I.W.F.* I have inquired further in the matter and find—the door is not completely closed. It is possible that in another couple of weeks I can still have "Reflections" in your possession to read. Trust it be so.

Until a ruling by the Supreme Court 17 June 1970, certain books and magazines were not permitted to us, and receiving or writing manuscripts or creating drawings for any purpose was totally prohibited. Today those restrictions are no longer active. We are permitted to subscribe to papers and magazines and to order books and certain "pornographic" materials.

*From 1968 until 18 October 1971, when the rule was struck down by the California Supreme Court, 25 percent of all monies accruing from creative endeavors of men on Death Row was withheld by the prison for use in the Inmate Welfare Fund, which benefits only prisoners outside the Row.

That ruling was very significant, inasmuch as it gave us condemned men an opportunity to try to help ourselves, our beloved ones and friends; it avails us the opportunity to express our emotions, thoughts and conclusions in respect to many things, many subjects; and finally, it gives us an opportunity to feel less isolated from the world—more a part of the living even though condemned to death. It gave us mental channels of escape. Freedom . . . .

It has been my contention from the beginning that I am not guilty of the crime for which I stand condemned. I have also admitted that I am not without some degree of blame. I worked hard all my life, a poor man, but a proud man. But to be black, poor and proud in America means: to be a prey for prejudice and injustice. Yet, I have enjoyed briefly during my existence the elite of living that I desire for every black, minority and under-privileged person in this country, and in the whole wide world. I can profoundly appreciate it when you write: this "could-be-beautiful country." I have maintained the understanding, respect and devotion of my family—my daughters; and that, my friend, has been my deliverer from despair . . . my greatest inspiration.

I hope to have some letters, poems and drawings for you in the very near future. We had much confusion—conflicts, and a few cuttings—here on the Row this past week (I was not involved) which resulted in a big shake-down and shake-up! Anyway, wasn't able to get any works executed during all that chaos.

"Each man seeks his liberation in one way or another." Well spoken . . . .

Writings of Joshua Hill and Thomas "Doc" Varnum arrive. We meet several more times to go over material selecting letters and poems. Various obstacles slow down materials sent but eventually all works arrive. The book grows. Dovie introduces me to Dan Roberts. An ongoing communication is maintained, letters passing between us every few days. The project nears completion after seven months of editorial, legal and personal communication. We both take a breather. We meet again in June for photos and final touches on Dovie's manuscripts. It is the happiest and strangest editorial meeting I have ever participated in. We are both tired. It is a good and close feeling.

His growth and faith have helped create this book.

Life betrays us without cause
Answer or Reason,
But endure Faith in Tomorrow
Which is life's
Hidden Season . . .

Joshua Hill

JOSHUA HILL, alias "Devil Josh," A-89495, Death Row, San Quentin, is twenty-six, the youngest man in this book. He has been on Death Row since he was nineteen. He writes:

> I'm incapable of surrendering to Life peacefully. I leave that to those whom Life has granted peace. Actually, there's a bestial simplicity about me—a nitty-gritty primitiveness.... I'm a hopeless anachronism: the Naked Ape before horseless carriages, U.S. Steel, underarm deodorants, computers and the California Penal Code. Life to me has been nothing but an endless struggle for as long as I can remember, and the struggle has seeped into my blood and soul and the wires of my spine. I cannot imagine Life without a struggle. Nor can I imagine myself not struggling— whether it be rebelling against The Establishment, dealing with personal enemies and miscellaneous transgressors, or wrestling with my many private demons."

As Dovie Mathis, who selected the following material, mentioned: "He has the sort of appearance and reveals the kind of intelligence which one might discover on any highly acclaimed college campus, and which you would least expect to find on Death Row."

After reading Josh's material I wrote to tell him how much I liked his work and asked whether he wanted to reconsider anything he had written before it was finalized as part of the book, my concern being that certain passages might cause him trouble if read by those who hold life and death command over his future. I feared that his writings might adversely affect future possibilities for commutation or clemency hearings. He responded:

> What I have written is the way it is with me, and that's the way I'd like it to stand. As for any possible "grief" my occasional anti-establishment diatribes, proddings, and general irreverence might bring upon me in the future, they are totally irrelevant and immaterial to me. I pay heed to neither caution nor consequence. It's not a matter of moral courage or commitment to the truth, but rather a luxurious and profound indifference. Janis Joplin sang, "Freedom's just another word for nothing left to lose." Well, Stephen, I haven't had anything to lose in a long, long time, so in some respects that makes me free ....

The Death of Sareta

Joshua Hill

I was reading the *Examiner* yesterday when I came across Sareta's picture. She was a fine little girl I used to know from South Philly: a really knocked-out little fox, about five feet tall but all heart. She was the type who would make a dude feel real protective, but at the same time, you know, when the chips were down, she would be one hell of a gun-moll. All heart.

Somebody had stabbed the broad to death. Cut her right there in the streets of South Philly with a butcher knife.

Allow me to take you on this semi-profound trip about what really gets to me about the way Sareta checked out. Here we have "Strump," a frail little girl who is about as violent as a rose petal, strolling down Reed Street in South Philly when, Zap! Some dude sticks her a couple of times, and it's all over with. Zap! Sareta checks out. It was probably the first time in her life she was ever exposed to any real danger, and yet that was enough to make her bite the dust. Meanwhile, on the other hand, here I am scribbling away with my little pen, strong and healthy as a young bull. Me: Mad Dog Vito, the Philadelphia wildman.

For my age, I've probably lived one of the most violent lives imaginable. I've been shot at twice and cut three times: furthermore, I've been hit with blackjacks, clubs, baseball bats, sticks, bricks, wine bottles and many other things. Also, I have participated in at least a dozen gang wars, and so many fights I lost count years ago. Not only that, but I was put under a death sentence two months before Strump even graduated from high school. Yet, despite all of this, I am still very much alive. That's an enormous thing, a very enormous thing. It's enough to make a young man stop and think. Know what I mean?

Three Letters
to Cathy in the Desert

FIRST LETTER

20 March 70

Hello, baby. I'm scribing you from the holding tank behind the Kangaroo Court in which I'm presently being railroaded. There is no one else in here now, and it feels sort of luxurious having so much room to myself for a change. But it's a luxury I'd gladly forego if I could have you here with me . . . .

There's a very large window in this tank. It's barred, of course, but you can look outside and see the free world. I've spent hours gazing down at the streets eight stories below and immersing myself in memories and fantasies. I'm beginning to trip so often these days it's difficult at times to distinguish reality from imagination. Know what I mean? But I suppose it really doesn't matter anyway, so what the hell.

A building is under construction right across the street, and it appears to grow taller every day. Like a young sapling. The men working on it resemble ants crawling all over the building's skeleton and zipping around busily doing their thing. Sort of weird and depressing, these men. At work they sweat and grunt and get dirty and punch time clocks and carry lunch pails and wear those utterly ridiculous-looking construction helmets. After work they go home, eat some kind of nauseating meal such as cornbeef & cabbage, drink a few beers, put their foot in little Jimmy's ass for being a bad boy in school, watch TV, and then rut away on their fat little wives for a while, before finally going to sleep—without having opened their eyes one time all day, or having had one interesting thought. And yet, in spite of all that humdrum mediocrity, there is much about their lives which I envy. Revolting, isn't it? I must be losing my mind.)

I've been reflecting upon the happenings of this past week in court. So far, my trial has been nothing more than a series of worsening disasters. Every day is a brand-new traumatic experience. But you know what, Cathy? After what I've been through these past six years there's nothing in this world anyone can do to Devil Josh. And that includes Round Roger (he's the prosecutor... bears a striking resemblance to a stuffed sausage), Judge Kathleen, those sick goddam cops who have been lying their asses off, and the State of California. Fuck 'em all, man. In fact, FUCK THE WORLD.

21 March 70

Hello, precious one. Are you hip to SILENCE? There is nothing more quiet than a prison at night after everyone is asleep. I used to stay up all night sometimes when I was still on the Row, and at about two o'clock in the morning everything would become absolutely silent—as if everyone were already dead. It would be so quiet I could hear my heart thumping like a drunken Indian pounding wildly on a tom-tom drum. Know what I mean? A very weird trip. And it's the same way here. I'm writing this letter at about three a.m., and it's so quiet that the sound of my breathing is like the wind rushing across the desert. Can you dig it?

Since sleep appears determined to elude me tonight, let me take you on a trip, baby. When I was seven years old I had a groovy little bike—a J.C. Higgins 24-incher. Say, Cathy, Devil Josh really loved that bike. Know what I mean? It was beautiful. Anyway, along with the bike, I had a little partner named Bobby, and I used to hop on my J. C. Higgins and make it over to Bobby's all the time. But in order to reach my partner's house I'd have to ride past this certain pad. And every time I rode past this certain pad a great big nasty ol' dog would ambush me. Boy, he was a big motherfucker, Cathy. He'd come tearing off that front porch every time I rode by and snap at my legs and rip the bottoms of my pants and chase me down the street for about a block and just scare the living hell right out of me. Wow. But one day I decided I'd had enough of that nasty ol' dog, so when he started chasing me I just stomped on the brake and brought my little J.C. Higgins to a screeching halt. Well, when I did that, the dog didn't do a damn thing but stand there snarling at me. So I just snarled right back for a few seconds; then I ran forward and tried to kick him. Boy, you should've seen that ol' sissy dog run! He hightailed it back to his porch like some weasel being shot at by a farmer. After that, he never bothered me at all. He wouldn't even bark anymore. Most animals are like that, I suppose—including humans. In fact, you know what? Sometimes when I'm thinking about that nasty ol' dog I sort of compare him to The Man. In a way, they're exactly the same.

Well, I think I'll check out now. The Sandman is beginning to lean on me. Besides, the sooner I get to sleep, the sooner I'll be able to have fantastic dreams about your healthy young body . . . .

23 March 70

What a gas! There's a dude here in the holding tank with me right now. Postelle (the bailiff) brought him in about five minutes ago. He's pacing up and down in front of me like some kind of maniac—sort of spastic and wild-eyed. Maybe he has to take a piss or something. Once in a while the dude looks over to see if I'm watching him. Weird. The guy tried to start a conversation with me when he first came in but I ignored him. I can tell all he wants to do is snivel about his beef—which is probably nothing more than a lightweight forgery. Fuck all that. The last thing in the world I need right now is listening to some sick motherfucker snivel about a lousy little forgery beef. Oh, oh. I don't believe it. This fool just laid down on the bench about three feet away from me. He's all propped up with his legs folded like a broad or something. Dizzy goddam knickknack. Wow. There sure are a lot of weird people in the world.

Meanwhile, I just found out that Madorid isn't going to testify in my behalf the way he promised last week. In case you've forgotten, Madorid is the dude I told you about several days ago—my rat-ass former codefendant. He took the witness stand during my last trial and assisted the district attorney in putting my partner Frank and me on Death Row. This time, however, he was going to straighten up his hand and do right; but Round Roger had him called out the other day for a little conference. Now the punk isn't going to testify. Which blows a major part of my defense. Madorid sent me word this morning that Round Roger had a member of the Adult Authority with him, and that the dude said he could forget about a parole if he testified in my behalf. Cold-blooded, ain't they? There is much evil in the state of California. But the coldest thing about the whole scene is the fact that all I wanted Madorid to do was tell the TRUTH. Just that, Cathy.

LATER ON . . . . Well, I'm sitting here in court listening to that stupid tape again. What a bummer. As soon as it began I picked up my pencil and started writing once more. Fuck that tape, man—it brings back too many bad echoes from the Past. I have nightmares about the goddam thing. It's hard to believe I was actually that sick at one time. And crazy. I'm beginning to understand why my first attorney wanted to have me committed to a mental institution.

26 March 70

I remember how I used to handle bummers when I was a kid. People would come around trying to put all their happiness off on me—as if their happiness would somehow compromise my sadness. I'd try to smile and put myself through changes and front off for them until they got out of my face—just to make them feel like they did something. Know what I mean? And besides, the sooner they got out of my face, the sooner I could concentrate on my problems and make everything right again. But all that is in the Past. I don't let anyone put his happiness off on me any more, Cathy—which is why you couldn't bring a smile to my lips last night. But fuck all that.

Wow, man, today is beautiful—dark and cold and damp and sinister. Heavy weather, man. Heavy. This is the type of day on which I'd like to put on my trenchcoat and stalk the streets of town, digging on the people. They shiver, Cathy—they shiver and huddle and scurry down the street all hunched over and everything. And then they hustle into those little restaurants and coffee shops for some warmth and social reassurance. But they always have to come out again. And it's always a little darker and a little colder and a little more sinister when they do. You know what, Cathy? I've noticed that this type of weather seems to bring out the fear and temerity in people. In the end we're all at the mercy of Mother Nature. It's quite a trip when you groove on it for a while.

Oh, oh. Here comes the bailiff right now, so I guess it's time for court to begin. I wonder what Kathleen and the DA have cooked up for me this time. It's no big thing whatever it is. They never get to Devil Josh no matter how bad they gang up on him. When a man has been down as long as I have and really doesn't give a fuck anymore, what can a twisted old woman and a rotund little Bircher do to him? Besides get him another death penalty, I mean.

All right, the time has come now for some Devil Josh Poetry. Are you ready for that? Okay, this first poem was written on the Row about a week before my one and only Execution Date (29 August 1967).

I've Been There Before

We used to watch him strolling
Up and down the tier,
His lively footsteps falling
From the front back to the rear.

He'd look at everybody
With a grin upon his face
And it seemed like he was happy
To be here in this place.

And if you were to ask him
About that smile he wore
He'd say "I keep on smiling
'Cause I've been there before."

We'd ask him to explain himself
But all he'd do was grin
So no one knew the secret
Of where it was he'd been.

Well, he was executed
Just the other day
And I heard he kept on smiling
In that same familiar way.

I also heard he whispered
As they closed the Chamber door
"Death ain't nothing to me
'Cause I've been there before."

This second poem is a little more intimate because—well, you'll
see.

Desert Flower

From the heat
And dust and sand
Came one soft and velvet flower
With beauty, love and power
Which lasted but one hour
Then crumbled
In my hand.

Well, what do you think of them? Personally, I think my
poetry bag is in desperate straits—but I hope they turn you on
in one way or another.

Say, baby, would you like to hear something ridiculous
that's been bugging me periodically for twenty years now?
You'll probably think I'm pretty stupid but I'll run it down

anyway. When I was five years old my family lived for a while in the backwoods of Virginia with my grandparents. Well, while we were staying there a family reunion was held at the pad, and about six million of my relatives came and stayed for a week or so. Well, ALMOST six million. Anyway, one of the relatives who came was my cousin, Jerry, who was the same age as I. And you know what Cousin Jerry brought with him? A motorboat. Boy, I'll never forget that motorboat. It was the most groovy toy I'd ever seen up to that time. The boat was yellow and blue and made out of tin, and it had a real propeller. All you had to do was wind the propeller, flip a switch, and the motor would run for five minutes. Jerry, who was a rotten little bastard at times, would never let me play with the motorboat. He'd wind the motor up and let it run right before my very eyes, but he'd never let me play with it. And he'd never put the boat in water. There was a giant marsh right near the pad, but Jerry never gave that boat a chance to float. He'd wind that propeller up and just let the motor run out while holding it in his hand. To me, that was just about the dumbest thing I'd ever seen in my brief existence. I mean, even at that age I was hip enough to know that boats are supposed to be in water. And I wanted to see that little boat floating so bad I didn't know what to do. Finally, I couldn't take it any longer. One day I punched Jerry right in the mouth; then I took the boat and ran toward the other end of the marsh. Well, right away Jerry went inside the pad and ratted on me, so in just a couple of minutes I had six million people coming after me. Boy, did that look weird. When I finally got to the other side, I wound the propeller up, flipped the switch and then gently put the boat in the water. And you know what? The stupid thing sunk immediately, man. The very instant I took my hand away that boat went straight to the bottom. I was so shocked I just knelt there looking down at the water until everyone caught up to me. My mother beat the fuck out of me when we got back to the pad, but I hardly even noticed it because my little mind was so busy trying to figure out why that dumb boat sunk. I mean, why would anyone make a boat that couldn't float? Sometimes I'll think about that incident when a certain thing happens which I can't understand. Like the time I went into a liquor store to buy some cigarettes and beer, and ended up with this hot murder beef . . . .

SECOND LETTER

11 April 70

Well, it's all over now except for closing arguments, which will take place after the noon recess. I'm not the slightest bit prepared for pleading my case, man. I haven't rehearsed anything, and there are no words in my head. I'm sort of like someone about to fight two dinosaurs with an empty squirt-gun. But it feels good. It feels so goddam good. Because I'm always at my best when I'm going for what I know with nothing in my head from in front. Wow, I'm really turned on right now. I wish you were here so we could groove.

Listen, before I carry this any further, I want to express how beautiful you were the other day when you made it possible for Wicked Willie to testify in my behalf. I know I've already expressed myself with my lips, but I've always felt that words are more sincere when they flow through a pen. Many hollow words are spoken through plastic lips. In any case, I love you, Cathy—in my own particular way. Not merely because you took care of business on Tuesday afternoon, of course, but also for countless other reasons which would probably take me an eternity to enumerate.

Oh, oh. I hear the rattling of keys again—which means Postelle is coming to take me away. Wow, man, I'm so turned on now I feel dizzy . . . .

12 April 70

I've been reflecting on the closing argument I made to the jury yesterday afternoon. It was quite a performance from what I've been told, but I rarely believe what people tell me. They will definitely put a young man on. Just between you and me, I don't think the jury was moved in the slightest. Oh, they were probably impressed with my performance to a certain extent, but only in the way a hunter is impressed by the cunning of an animal he is about to shoot. Can you see where I'm at? They couldn't look me in the eyes, Cathy. Not one of them could look me in the eyes. I'm not sure they even heard my words—although it really doesn't matter one way or the other. Curiously enough, I felt sorry for them. In fact, I felt so sorry for the lames I actually ended up taking them off the hook completely: "Don't do me any favors. You haven't BEEN doing me any favors, so don't start NOW. Just do what you think is right and stand by it." That wasn't a very practical ploy, I must admit, but they seemèd so tiny and pathetic trying to avoid my eyes I just couldn't help displaying my own particular brand of compassion. And I just couldn't snivel to them. Can you see where I'm at, Cathy? I just couldn't snivel.

Incidentally, that actor was there again with his fine little companion. I call her Kewpie Doll. She seems to be favoring my side in this thing, although appearances can be deceiving. Anyway, I've been trying to decide whether or not I'd rather get down with the broad or just sort of cuddle her a little bit. She seems to touch the Big-Brother-and-Friend aspect of my personality rather than the Horny-Male-Animal aspect. All of which "must give me pause to reflect," as Shakespeare would say. You see, I've contracted a rabidly virile case of Spring Fever, and I usually want to sock it to everyone when I'm in the midst of one of my satyrmaniac episodes. Well, AL-MOST everyone . . . .

I've been contemplating some of our recent conversations. We've had some very interesting colloquies of late. I groove on them at night just before I drift off to sleep—examining, analyzing and all that. Heavy dialogues space me out. Do you remember what you told me concerning your parents? That REALLY started me tripping. The information you gave me changed my entire conception of your background. I thought you had been raised out in the desert by an old prospector or something. In reality, though, you had a fairly sophisticated upbringing. We are diametrical opposites in that respect. I was raised by common people in a very unsophisticated environment. In fact, now that I think about it, we're diametrical opposites in just about EVERY respect. Sort of like a hawk and a dove. I find it amazing that we have even a lightweight affinity for each other, considering our differences in attitude and life-style. Though what the hell all that has to do with anything is beyond me. But it does.

That was a very perceptive remark you made last week concerning the relationship between my sister and me, considering that you've never seen us together or anything. Misty and I are extremely tight, despite the fact that we grew up at each other's side. I suppose that's a somewhat peculiar thing to say, but looking back I can think of no other way to phrase it. There was a time when I would've done just about anything in the world for the little broad. And I probably still would, although I'm not as certain of that as I once was. I mean, realistically speaking, we are hardly more than strangers to each other now. While I've been rotting away in this wretched world of cold steel bars and utter madness, Time has taken the girl I grew up with and made her a woman—a woman with a husband, a child and a life of her own. A life as alien to the existence I lead as mercy was to the Spanish Inquisition. When I heard the news of Misty's marriage I immediately felt as if some mysterious bond which held us together had been severed. Know what I mean? In other words, to reverse an old cliche, I lost a sister instead of gaining a brother-in-law. But that's enough about Misty, man. I haven't thought everything out yet where she's concerned.

Meanwhile, you've got to lighten up on me, baby! It just isn't fun to put on an act for a broad and then have her pull my covers. That's no way to treat Devil Josh. At least you could show me some consideration by PRETENDING to be taken in by my performances. That's the least you could do. After all, I've spent most of my life rehearsing those acts, and it's pretty traumatic having someone laugh at me and say, "Aw, Devil Josh, stop putting me on!" when I'm right in the middle of one of my favorite exhibitions. It's very disconcerting. I feel psychologically naked when a person sees through one of my acts. And I'm sure you realize what THAT means . . . .

Wow, what a trip! I'm sitting here in court right this very moment, intermittently scribbling lines to you and checking out the jury. Kathleen is reading the instructions and her voice drones on like the sound of a muffled outboard motor: "Murder is the unlawful killing of a human being with malice aforethought . . . ." Once in a while Kathleen murmurs the word DEATH and when she does I watch the eyes of my jury (I'm in a very dramatic mood today). Only two of them can even glance my way: Sweaty and Arnold. It's strange that these people find looking into my eyes so difficult. I first noticed it when I was testifying on the witness stand last week and I've been aware of it ever since. This idiosyncrasy of theirs is very intriguing. If I didn't know better I'd say they are extremely reluctant to kill me—that they find taking a man's life repugnant. If such is the case, it's quite a contradiction to their own personal lives. After all, they give money to the government each year so Uncle Sam can make bombs to drop on skinny little yellow people who have never done them any harm. If that isn't killing I don't know what is. Or they raise their sons on apple pie and Hollywood war movies for eighteen years, then let Uncle Sam put uniforms on the poor little bastards and send them off to a country they don't even belong in to get blown away. It's all the same, and the trip has no end. Their unawareness nauseates me, and I feel degraded being judged by people who haven't the heart to look into my eyes.

By the way, have I ever told you that I was in the Army at one time? Well, I was, and I'm proud to say I served my country with honor: I went A W O L before Uncle Sam could send me across the waters to kill and mangle people who've never done me wrong, in a land I have no right to invade. That's about the only thing I've ever done in my entire life that has any real merit.

The district attorney has been acting strangely these past few days. Friday afternoon, at the end of my performance, he said, "That was a very good argument, Mr. Hill." Which shocked the hell out of me because we've been at each other's throat ever since this trial began. In fact, I was so startled when he said that that all I could do was stare at him in the same manner I would a water buffalo doing push-ups. But that isn't half of it. This morning when I came to court he showed me copies of the instructions he planned to have Kathleen read to the jury. A substantial number of these instructions were actually more beneficial to the defense than the prosecution. Then to top it all off, he asked Kathleen to give an alibi instruction concerning an assault that was introduced against me at the trial. The sonofabitch was actually trying to help me! Where will it all end? I've come to the conclusion that the man has either taken complete leave of his senses, or he actually possesses a sense of justice and fair play. It just HAS to be a mental breakdown of some sort. I simply refuse to believe there is such a thing as a district attorney with a sense of justice and fair play. It disturbs my conception of American jurisprudence and humanity in general. I mean, everyone knows that district attorneys fabricate evidence, collaborate with prosecution witnesses and just do anything they possibly can to get a defendant killed or thrown in prison. Everyone knows that.

Meanwhile, do you still think you're pregnant? Your chest definitely was far out the last time you showed it to me. Say, Cathy, are you going to drop the little stranger in a hospital, or do you plan a natural childbirth out there in the desert? Among the coyotes and rattlers and lizards and tumbleweed and cacti. You know what, Cathy? I saw a semi-natural childbirth one time and actually assisted in it partially. That was one of the most disturbing experiences of my entire life. I was eighteen at the time and slightly demented—which probably had something to do with the profound effect the experience exerted upon my mind. Anyway, I don't think I'll ever forget the way that baby looked when it first left his mama's womb.

So tiny and helpless and ugly and soft and vulnerable—oh so very fucking vulnerable. Man, I wanted to hold that little kid in my arms and protect it from the world and just never let it go. Know what I mean? That was probably the closest I'll ever come to understanding what it's like to be a father.

Wait a minute. It just occurred to me why the district attorney was so liberal and conscientious about those jury instructions. The little sausage-head motherfucker wanted to make sure no kind of error was made which could be attacked on appeal. I don't know what came over me, thinking that lousy pig Bircher had assumed a sense of justice and fair play. I must've been on some kind of weird trip . . . .

14 April 70

I'm sitting here in my cell thinking about the jury and trying to decide whether or not to jerk off. Naturally the two thoughts are unrelated. Anyway, my judges went out yesterday and they have yet to return. Which surprises me. This morning they asked to have certain parts of my testimony read to them, so apparently they're taking their responsibility as jurors somewhat seriously. I find that slightly amazing.

And now, since I can think of nothing else to write, let me conjure up some Devil Josh Poetry. Provided I can think of something to inspire my pen. Let me see. Oh, yes. Here's a mini-poem about your eyes:

Childish Blue

Laughing light blue magic
Watching me with love and joy
But seeing MAN instead of BOY
And wishing that weren't true,
Those eyes of childish blue . . .

Sort of brief and slightly mysterious, but I hope you like it anyway. I suppose I'm not really in the mood to compose at the present time.

Man, do I ever need a woman right now.

Well, baby, Devil Josh has been downed again. The jury came in just before noon with the verdict. Curiously enough, I felt no emotion at all other than a slight embarrassment at having lost a battle. It was really quite a trip. You should've seen the way they fronted off and everything—grave, regretful and sadly firm. Like a farmer about to shoot his favorite plowhorse because it has a broken leg. One of them even went so far as to shed a tear. That was Grace—who, by the way, gives me a very strange feeling. All in all, I'd have to say they put on a very good act. In fact, just between you and me, I had the insane and overwhelming urge to applaud. I've always been appreciative of a good performance. You know what, Cathy? Sometimes I honestly believe there's something wrong with me.

Well, I think I'll split for now and devote my thoughts entirely to something frivolous and pornographic. Or maybe I'll type up what I've written so far and have it smuggled out to you. In any event—'bye . . . .

PS: Here's a poem that just now flooded into my head like sunlight flooding into a dark cave. I hope you don't find it too nauseating—it's sort of on the dramatic side, I suppose.

I've Had Mine

One morning is every dawn
Since the beginning of Time
And one night is every darkness
Since the birth of stars
One drop of rain is an
Ocean from the heavens
And an ocean is nothing more
Than a raindrop tasting of salt
One small rock is every mountain
That has ever kissed a cloud
And one grain of sand is
All of Mother Earth
Just one time is Forever
And I've had mine once.

THIRD LETTER

It is the silent hours between midnight and dawn as I begin this letter. Quiet and cool. There's a blanket across my shoulders, hiding my body from the night chill. Have you noticed how cold it's been lately? Like the afterbreath of Winter. The only time I've felt warm these past few weeks is when you smile . . . .

I've been contemplating my Monday Night Flight. To be completely honest, I'm sort of shocked at what I saw inside during that magic carpet ride. There is much evil lurking in Devil Josh. And madness. Insanity thrashes around in my head like a shark trapped in a bathtub. Where does it all come from, Cathy? Wicked Willie told me yesterday that I'd better not fuck with LSD anymore because I can't handle it under these circumstances. Perhaps the dude is right. But naturally I'm not going to follow his advice. It was too interesting an experience for me to limit myself to just one trip. Wicked Willie definitely does have a point though. Would you believe I got into three hassles when I got loaded? I got into three hassles, and kissed a young kid behind the ear. That isn't my bag usually but I could've sworn that kid was a girl I used to know back in Philadelphia. Maybe it was his shoulder-length hair and everything.

Yesterday and the day before were really far out, man. I was taken to the LCMC clinic for an examination of my nose. An open reduction shall be performed on May 1. I was overtaken by a very peculiar sensation when the doctor informed me he was going to operate. I had the sudden and inexplicable urge to talk him out of it—which is definitely weird considering how paranoid I've been about the stupid thing these past five months. Very strange.

So you've fallen madly in love with me, huh? Well, well, well. What do you know about that. Needless to say, I dig the idea of you being madly in love with me and all that, but frankly, I don't believe it's true—for two reasons. First of all, you've got a severely retarded pair-bond instinct; and secondly, I'm just not the type of dude a girl like you falls madly in love with. Know what I mean? I think you're on some kind of trip, Cathy. I really do.

Jesus, my left nut is still killing me. Would you believe it's about the size of a tennis ball? If I'm lying, I'm flying. A fleshy, black and blue tennis ball.

29 April 70

Now see that?—I went and did it again. I don't know, Cathy. I guess I'm just a cad, a scoundrel and an all-around beast, that's all. Every time you come visit me I tell myself, "Devil Josh, you better smile for this little fox 'cause she's someone special." Unfortunately, however, there are moments when I forget myself. Like this afternoon, for example. What can I say?

It continually amazes me how diverse some of our views are. As well as our understanding of what we see. Where did you get your eyes? Perhaps it's our difference in ages. Five years can mean a lot. Anyway, about the only thing we agree on is that we dig each other. Which is all that really matters, I suppose. You know what, Cathy? The most perplexing aspect about our difference in attitude is that you have so much faith and I have none at all. I mean, what do you see that I don't see, or what do I see that you don't see? It's all very complicated, and the answer probably lies somewhere in the heart of experience.

Meanwhile, looking back at my trial in analytical retrospect, it appears I committed three fatal blunders. The first, and most grave, was not disqualifying Judge Kathleen under 170.6 of the Penal Code at the very outset. But of course I had no idea what a monster she'd turn out to be in the end because she did such a truly remarkable job of masquerading her real attitude towards me during our pretrial encounters. Why, Kathleen's act was so convincing that I was actually under the impression I would receive a fair and impartial trial up until the second day of proceedings. Which is sort of tantamount to a lamb believing it has been invited to a lion's den to watch television. My second fatal blunder was calling convicts to testify in my behalf. At the time I felt it was absolutely necessary for me to call witnesses in order to negate, neutralize and mitigate certain evidence introduced against me concerning my conduct on the Row. But I realize now that it was a mistake of the highest degree to let certain individuals take the stand. Unfortunately, I had no conception of the enormity of the error until my last witness was testifying and I noticed a juror subjecting him to the same type of stares an Israeli soldier in Cairo might receive. Cathy, I've come to the conclusion that prison life, in SOME cases, seriously detracts from one's savoir faire. I've also concluded that after doing several years behind the walls some individuals' ideas of proper courtroom decorum become severely distorted. Like when Wicked Willie gave Round Roger the finger. Or the time Tank demolished the microphone he was given to put around his neck and then almost jumped on Postelle. And then there were the outbursts by Mosca and Animal Jack. Jesus Christ. My final blunder was refusing to snivel. What can I say? I suppose there are many things in life which I can do fairly well, but one of them is NOT sniveling. Other than all that, I hardly made any mistakes at all . . . .

Here's a little verse before I enter the land of dreams—where nothing's what it seems.

Observation

I've seen Yesterdays
Become Tomorrows
And watched Forever
Pass between them . . . .

30 April 70

I'm scribing you from the hospital right now. LCMC. The

Man came and kidnapped me while I was on the phone rapping to Gypsy. They've settled me in a large room by myself with a groovy view. I'm thirteen stories up. Tomorrow morning I'll watch the sun rise. Whoopee. I may just masturbate. It's been a long, long time since I've seen a sunrise. Incidentally, Gypsy told me you were doing something very important. You'll have to run it down the next time we're together. My curiosity is running wild. Like a pack of wolves in the desert.

Meanwhile, there is hope for my left nut! A doctor examined me about twenty minutes ago and said there is nothing unusual in the changes the poor thing has gone through considering I was kicked in it. He assured me that it won't be long before my left nut is just like my right one again. My mind is now at ease.

Oh, oh. I don't believe it! A nurse gave me something to make me sleep a few minutes ago and it's getting me loaded! I'm feeling a rush and everything! Wow. Spinning, spinning, spinning, and my bed looks absolutely beautiful. Bye . . . .

1 May 70

There is much disappointment in a California sunrise. It's sort of like watching a pregnant red basketball rising from the bottom of a swimming pool. I attempted to write some verse, but found the whole event so uninspiring that I couldn't think of any lines worth dulling the tip of my pencil for. However, I was able to conjure up something for the month of May. No, that isn't true. Actually, the poem concerns itself with a time of life rather than the month of May per se. I'd lay the stupid thing on you but it's much too disgusting. And personal. I've had a morbid kind of preoccupation with Time lately. The past six years I've spent behind bars are beginning to weigh heavily upon my mind. If a man could be young twice, this portion the state of California has taken from my life wouldn't be such a great loss. But Father Time just isn't that generous, and what has gone so far is gone forever. Like an amputated leg. There are moments when I feel like a blind child trying to see a rainbow, or a deaf-mute attempting to speak to a lovely woman: sort of hopeless and futile. Know what I mean? But don't get me wrong.

Meanwhile, it's very warm this morning. Perhaps spring has finally arrived. I can feel my body expanding the way it always does during warm weather. And I feel extremely passionate and sensual. I wish you were here beside me . . . .

3 May 70

Well, I'm back at the jail and my nose didn't go through any changes on Friday the way it was supposed to. The doctor who was to assist in the operation suffered a death in his family and had to be excused. It's very doubtful that business will be taken care of between now and the eighth, which is when I'm going back north, so I'll probably never get the sonofabitch fixed. A man isn't given any extensive medical treatment on the Row because the doctors at Quentin think it would be a waste of time, energy and expense, since there's a possibility you might be executed and everything. Know what I mean? I really don't give a fuck anyway though, so what the hell. No, that isn't true. I really DO give a fuck, but I'll probably get over it someday. You know, it's strange that someone should die on that particular day. Not only because I was scheduled for surgery, but also because Friday was so very beautiful. When Doctor Melgard broke the news to me I remember looking out the window and thinking how incongruous it was that someone had died on such an exquisite morning. As incongruous as a child choking to death on his own birthday cake.

But fuck all that. Let me write you a poem. It just occurred to me that I'll be leaving before the week has ended and our visits shall become a thing of the past. So let me conjure up a few appropriate lines: "some simple, heartfelt lay," as Longfellow would say.

Glad We Met

There is much I would change
And rearrange
Between what is now
And what has gone before
But you I would keep the same
And it's a shame
That Life won't give us more
Than Time will presently allow.

5 May 70

Black Tuesday. The store man didn't bring any candy and peanuts to sell this morning and a lot of dudes are beginning to panic, since they cannot subsist on the slop doled out at meal times. Many people depend on candy and peanuts for their very sustenance. Poor devils. Some of them are talking suicide. I can see the newspapers now:

46 INMATES COMMIT SUICIDE IN THE COUNTY JAIL

Forty-six inmates at the Los Angeles County Jail committed suicide today because there was no candy or peanuts available for them to buy. Names are being withheld pending notification of relatives.

Jail officials stated the majority of the victims either cut their wrists or hung themselves. However, two men were drowned attempting to flush themselves down their toilets. Also, one man died as a result of having his genitals bitten off after attacking a group of sixteen deputies, and one other inmate died of a fatal overdose of corn-beef at dinner.

Mayor Samuel Yorty ("Mayor Sam") has termed the Jail a disaster area, and for reasons known only to himself, declared Martial Law.

Sheriff Peter J. Pitchess ("Sheriff Pete"), in an effort to put an end to the serious outbreak of suicides ("It ain't natural and it's bad for morale"), has ordered his men to roam the jail shooting any inmate caught trying to take his own life.

Well, I think I'll bring this madness to an end, baby. I probably won't sock it to you again until I get back north. Writing from the Row is going to be a drag because I won't be able to have as much freedom in expressing myself as I do when I smuggle my scribes out to you. And they definitely will short-stop any poems I try to mail out. You know how pigs are. Listen, take care of yourself. And if you get a chance, think about me once in a while.

Thomas L. Varnum

THOMAS L. "DOC" VARNUM, *B-2449-A, Death Row, San Quentin, California, is introduced by his best friend Dovie Carl Mathis, A-84403, who selected his material from Doc's forthcoming book,* An Era of Dissent: A Personal View.

During my more than seven years on Death Row, Thomas, my next-door neighbor, became my closest, dearest and devoted friend. I gave him the nickname of "Doc" because of his self-acquired medical knowledge, and because of his remarkable resemblance to the legendary Doc Holliday! Doc is a black man whose shade of skin earned him the alias "Golden God": sometimes a bit cynical but always honest, open and outspoken; a man who respects the opinions of other men, who has won the respect and trust of more condemned inmates than any other black man on Death Row.

I have never taken the liberty of questioning him with regard to the details of the crimes for which he was convicted and condemned. However, the crime of robbery and murder allegedly occurred around the hour of six thirty on the evening of 14 August 1962. He was tried and convicted in a superior court in the county of Los Angeles, California, along with two codefendants, on 19 December 1962. The codefendants received a reward of life imprisonment while the same judge and jury elected to make Thomas L. Varnum society's scapegoat—therefore sentenced him to be sacrificed to the grim and grisly finality of California's lethal gas chamber, which clearly illustrates ambiguous and arbitrary application of American "justice." This is just another among the many cases where defendants in capital punishment cases are tried and convicted on the very same charge or charges—yet one is sentenced to lesser punishment, life imprisonment, while the other is sentenced to suffer the supreme penalty of death. However, hope is with me that the state shall not succeed in this case!

I am proud and privileged to introduce you to this man through the reflections of his beautiful and sensitive soul.

Dovie Carl Mathis

Poems

Thomas L. Varnum

During the span of my life I have loved many things; I have loved life as life has loved me. But now, I am but a living page in a book that was once a story—nothing but vague words with complicated meanings that only a few people understand. On this day, I meditate upon a past where faces and memories puzzle me. I look upon them as an old man who sees that his youth has fled like the winds of time only to be reminded that on the morrow when he awakes he must face another day of loneliness, gloom, and despair.

As I sit here confined in this dark cell whose walls bruise my aching heart, I feel like a river that runs but will never reach the sea. My heart is saddened by those who gaze upon me and say, "You must have hope." What do I care about hope? My heart and soul cry only for justice.

I have thought of death as a means of replacing this heavy and tiring burden that I carry upon my shoulders. I do not speak of killing myself, but view it as a means of eternal peace. Is there not peace in death? For in death, one will not feel the pains or the sorrows that live with a man from the time that he is born.

The world in which I live is a very small one where one does not hear the humming of bees or the laughter of small children, nor see the sun or feel its warmth upon one's face. I even feel at times like a field of corn amidst a drought, doomed to die without water. I have suffered in a million ways and died a thousand deaths, and yet there is the will of my soul to go on. For I know that the night and its darkness and the sleep that comes with it is going to take this pain that I have kept for so long . . . .

YESTERDAYS

Our tomorrows are gone like
    the winds of time, through
thought and rhyme.

THE BLACK EARTH

A great blackness covered the earth
like a mantle of soft summer silence.

The land was void and empty of Life—
except for the black bubbling of the
mud which seeped from the black crust.

Suddenly, from the formless and black
sky came a shining shaft of light to
the black mud below stirring it to life.

The mud moved, twisted, and formed a
strong black body with hands reaching
out to that shaft of light above.

A booming voice shattering the night
called out to the now stilled black
form in the mud commanding it to rise
and stand in the glory of blackness.

The Black Man was created! He would
rule the empires of Time and fall prey
to them who would claim all the world
was theirs by right of their color.

Blackness was chained, sold, bled,
and cast into the dungeons of Time to
decay and die without a trace of real
Existence to the color-mind of Mankind
who deems that He is God of the Earth.

Yet, blackness stood Proud like a true
seasoned warrior through the blood of
many Tribulations and to emerge Golden
and Victorious from the Battle's Time!

BLACK BLACKNESS

A Black mind begins to sleep
taking with it a Day's pains
that cannot seep

Deeper and deeper into
the Black pit of Night
where no worries come to haunt you
while you make your silent flight

Now come faded Black dreams
with ghouls and demons
who will laugh over lost Black reasons
and awryed Black schemes

Sleep on Black restless mind
and maybe in your Black slumber
You just might find
the answer to the Riddle that
binds your Blackness in Time

I DON'T KNOW

What is this Madness that grips my Soul?
What is Love with an evil woman?
What is Tomorrow to a Fool who missed Today?
What is Rain to a Hand which cannot Feel it?
What is Time to One who cannot See it?
What is Life to a Tree that Bears no Fruit?
What is a Heart without a Soul?
　　　　I don't know, I don't know

What is the reflection of Time when there is no Time?
What is Black is Black, but what is White is not White?
What is a Book with no Words on its Pages?
What is Angela Davis Thinking about?
What is Justice to One who cannot Buy it?
What is Laughter without Sound?
What is an Indian without His Lance?
　　　　I don't know, I don't know

What is a Lie and What is Truth?
What is a Shapely Hip to a Blind Man?
What is Wine to a Wino?
What is Sex to a Homosexual?
What is a Spider to a Fly?
What is Knowledge without Motivation and Purpose?
What is a Breast to a hungry Lip?
　　　　I don't know, I don't know

What is a Pen without Ink?
What is Green but is not Grass?
What is a Dictionary without Definition?
What is Agnew trying to Hide?
What is Revolution without Blood?
What is Understanding without Understanding?
What is Black Desire without Black Fire?
　　　　I don't know, I don't know

MEMORIES

What are memories?
Are they painful arrows, our
yesterdays? Or are they
moments of some sweetness that
we no longer possess?
Tell me, what are memories?

MARY—A BLACK ANGEL

She was Black like the Pit of Night
With penetrating eyes
Clear as Nature's crystals
And just as Bright
           A Black Angel

Her voice was soft and gentle like
A lazy Summer stream
But it could at Times be Mysterious
And sensuous as some faded and
Forgotten Black dream
           A Black Angel

Sweet like April's rain
When into my life She came
Filling it With Love and Joy
While easing my burden and Pain
           A Black Angel

She was not from the Sky above
But from the Black mud like me
When We met and Kissed
And fell in Love
           A Black Angel

LITTLE BLACK GIRL

Little Black girl playing
in the street
so innocent—pure and sweet
while running and dancing
with wings on Her feet

Not a care in the world
does She possess,
only Love and Goodwill
will She show at its best

I think just to see Her Smile
and laugh while She skips rope,
would lift a downtrodden heart
and raise a faded dream to new Hope.

Leaman Smith

LEAMAN SMITH, A-85506, Death Row, San Quentin, is an accomplished musician and analyst of the prison environment. His knowledge of the subject is all too extensive, paralleled only by the most veteran of his captors: the majority of his forty-one years has been spent behind prison walls. Through diligent study and practice he has taught himself to be proficient on several instruments, as too in later years he has educated himself generally through the study of law, English, literature, psychology and general semantics. But the greatest part of his preliminary education has been in criminal techniques, leading him from one penitentiary to another. His "schooling" began between the ages of eleven and eighteen in reformatories, and advanced through the tortuous "graduate schools" of Lewisberg, Atlanta, Leavenworth and Alcatraz.

Then with the approach of death came a new interest in life. During his more than seven years on Death Row much of Leaman's time has been given to "reprogramming" himself, literally re-arranging his consciousness. His reflections based on the principles of "psycho-cybernetics" and general semantics have produced a stability which, had it been obtained earlier in life, might have precluded his more than two decades of prison experience. But there was much to obstruct such growth, much early "mislearning." At first, even in prison, there were glimmerings of the man within. At twenty-one, while still in the Oklahoma state reformatory, he was offered a music scholarship by the University of Oklahoma, but the authorities had another future in mind for him and he was not allowed to accept. The glimmerings nearly went out. His "education" was directed toward other areas.

Leaman's constant search for knowledge has now led to a personal expansion. His calm analysis of the prison environment could be of immeasurable aid to those administrators who admit that prisons are becoming increasingly unmanageable, but he is locked away "on ice," unheard and disregarded, awaiting the final diploma of his prison education: execution.

Reflections of a Condemned Man

Leaman Smith

I have been confined on San Quentin's Death Row for seven years.

Existence on Death Row is difficult under the best of conditions. The environment is oppressive, repressive and abnormal. To maintain or regain mental balance is a constant struggle, an imperative. Whether or not by design, forces and conditions tending to undermine that imperative exist in abundance. But you must learn to adjust to this environment. Your whole mental well-being depends on it.

Fortunately, we are endowed with the capacity to adjust to the most difficult situations, and those persons unable to utilize this capacity populate the mental institutions. Often passage of time aids the adjustment, but on Death Row we have a distorted concept of time so more is demanded of us. Survival requires a conscious effort to occupy your mind completely—with something. It requires even more than that: it also requires adjustment to the closeness of a diverse and often divergent group of personalities.

I set about making my adjustment without plan. For the first few months some intense self-examination was in order since I had become reconciled to death. Much of what I learned about myself displeased me. This was a period of regretfully reviewing my life and realizing how it had been wasted. Why had it taken a death sentence to make me understand these things?

In the past there had always been the future glowing brightly, and this future became the focal point rather than the past. Facing what seemed to be an imminent death with an unknown future made it easier to think critically. Something triggered a desire for better self-understanding and a re-alignment of values before dying.

It is difficult to pinpoint just when this change of attitude occurred. I know that reading the transcripts of the trial was influential for they contained, in cold black and white print, evidence of faults and character deficiencies. Never before had they seemed so numerous. It is likely that the conscious desires for self-understanding began after reading and then recalling the expert psychiatric and psychological opinions about me. These opinions stated, in effect, that I could be expected to perform in the future as I had in the past. They cast doubt on my ability to set and work toward long-term goals, and they cast doubt on my ability to adjust to society.

This was a prognosis I learned to resent very much. I did not and do not believe the expert opinions. Every human being is a dynamic individual, a constantly changing individual. I resented, and still resent, the idea that someone else could predict my future, making me a static entity. Past conduct does not, will not, and cannot preclude my change and development. To disprove the experts became a challenge to me. I intend challenging till either I am executed or the experts change their opinions.

Whenever and however the desire for self-understanding and self-improvement began it must continue in this stifling environment, without prison-sanctioned assistance, if anything worthwhile is to be accomplished. This is in itself a challenge.

I have quit hiding my inadequacies with self-serving rationalizations. I now recognize them and have set about changing them. How can one go about this?

For me it was a combination of studying general semantics, law, psycho-cybernetics and human relations.

By studying general semantics I first became critical of the language patterns affecting my actions, as they affect everyone's actions. General semantics taught me to be conscious of the entire symbolic process, especially language, and how to avoid inappropriate responses to the daily barrage of words encountered not only through the mass media but through personal contacts. It provided a set of operational principles that permit more accurate evaluations of problems in life.

I believe the most important things law has taught me are the ability to reason and to think objectively. Except for professional people, I believe most of us have purely subjective reasoning processes about nearly everything touching our personal lives. We are basically concerned with nothing outside our small circles of close friends and relatives. When we think of law we think in terms of its application to protect our individual lives and property, and rarely are concerned with its application for 203 million people. When our property is not involved, we tend to consider laws restrictive and, therefore, an encroachment on personal freedom. (I intend no reference to the right of proper dissent.) The important thing is not simple agreement but to learn to think and exercise citizens' prerogatives in such a way that will benefit you as an individual and the society as a whole: to think and weigh and decide a certain question as objectively and reasonably as possible. This might sound very elementary. The underlying principles might even be common knowledge, though I doubt it. Still, it must be borne in mind that it was a defect in these thinking abilities that greatly contributed to, if it was not totally responsible for, my present situation. I cannot believe anyone without a defect of some sort would have persisted in conduct that ostracized him from all those things most cherished in life.

Part of what I have learned on Death Row can be termed self-understanding and the understanding of human relations. I do not concern myself about whether the term "human relations" meets the definition used by some experts in a particular field. I use the term to define my personal relationships with others and the self-understanding gained from these relationships.

Compelled closeness to others has been instrumental in affecting my attitudes about people. Each man has his personal battle to fight and win in his own way on the Row, but it is also necessary for him to fit into the daily life of those around him without creating undue friction—a neat trick when you consider the diversity of personalities involved. Certainly no one in normal society would find himself freely associating with personalities so dissimilar. It has been rewarding to learn not only how to live with these personalities but to like them. I have tried to learn from these men—mostly about myself. It has been said that we see ourselves mirrored in those around us; that we learn the characteristic traits we most dislike in ourselves by recognizing and disliking them in others. Not only do I want to get along with these men of dissimilar personality, I want to discover my own faults mirrored in them.

It disturbs me to see men waste this valuable opportunity to learn about themselves. I believe it stems more from an inability to know how to proceed than from any real disinterest. I doubt that any man up here is genuinely satisfied with the life he has led. I certainly am not.

It is not easy to accomplish anything on Death Row, and many fail or do nothing. I believe the men can honestly be grouped into three categories (admitting that men cannot at any time be easily categorized):

(1) those who actually deteriorate because of their inability to accept and adjust to the rigors reality now imposes upon them, and whose mental stability moves steadily toward an imbalance;
(2) those who do nothing to advance themselves in any way, either through inability or by so misdirecting their efforts that an impasse is reached; and, finally,
(3) those who are advancing themselves by expanding their capacity and ability to understand and correct their attitudes and antisocial conduct.

There are no trade training programs for men on Death Row to help them make these changes; there is no counseling and very little, if any, encouragement from the administration.

Whatever real advancement a condemned man makes must be in his personal attitudes and conduct.

Except for the opportunity for learning to exercise self-discipline, I have little confidence in the trade training programs as the ultimate in rehabilitation plans. I believe such programs are basically misdirected for overall effect. To attempt to solve a prisoner's problem and return him to society as a useful citizen merely by teaching him a trade completely overlooks or ignores the undeniable fact that such problems more often than not stem from the mind. Many men, including myself, could have earned a decent, respectable living plying their trades or otherwise utilizing their abilities. I have known men who took a new trade training program each time they were recommitted to prison. Their training did not prevent their anti-social (criminal) conduct.

In my estimation, teaching a man to understand and cope with himself and his relationship to society is the most effective way of rehabilitation.

My three categories of men are on a mental basis since that is our only real source of contact. The smallest group contains those few who suffer mental deterioration. Because the group is so small, I pay little attention to it. There is only a moral duty, granting that men on Death Row are still capable of recognizing and performing certain moral duties, to bring this obvious deterioration to the attention of some interested person who will then take more positive actions on their behalf. I have done this.

The larger group by far is the second group, those who accomplish nothing for various reasons. This failure is regretful, because many of these men require only sensible direction, given within a context which they can relate to their own lives and experiences. Within this group are those whose every wakened hour is an exercise in escapism: television, card games, checkers, etc. Were this not possible it is likely that many would belong in the first group. There is a valid and necessary need for diversion under these circumstances, but the time could be better spent.

I do not believe men learn useful mental skills or personal insight while maintaining secret thoughts. I have found that when you finally begin learning and understanding yourself you also develop an almost overwhelming desire to learn about other persons and things: to probe for approval and verification of what you have learned, and expound on the conclusions reached so as to make them a permanent part of your mental process by repetition. In short, you need sounding-boards outside your own mind, and those most readily available are the other men on Death Row. If you do not utilize them to better your self-understanding you are left to think your own thoughts without receiving either disapproval or verification. Correspondence with persons outside is too strictly limited and would not, in any event, be sufficient. Helpful, yes. Sufficient, no. Learning puts too many demands on correspondents. The average person must live from day to day struggling for his own existence and peace of mind. He neither has time nor inclination to answer a thousand questions even if he could. The mental exertion is too much to expect from an already burdened mind. No, there is not much assistance available. The basic answers must be found right here on the Row. Any other belief is pure delusion.

I consider myself in the third group, those who are learning something about themselves. I have learned a great deal about myself, not all bad, and those things candidly admitted to be faults are being overcome. Where I was emotionally immature, I am moving toward maturity; where I was intolerant of others, I have capitalized on the opportunity presented by the Row where there are many things to tolerate; where I was totally lacking in patience, I have developed a degree of patience that would have made a material difference in my life had it been possessed earlier; where I was thoughtless of the rights of others, I have learned to appreciate the fact that everyone has a right to live his life and maintain his possessions free from the danger of losing either by the actions of a thoughtless individual.

It naturally follows that an outgrowth of self-understanding will be learning to understand others. I have no doubt that my seven years on Death Row have done much to improve my attitudes and behavior toward other people.

Someone once said, "Many people go throughout life committing partial suicide—destroying their talents, energies, creative qualities. Indeed, to learn how to be good to oneself is often more difficult than to learn how to be good to others."

I believe that. I know the tragedy of my life is a result of mistreating myself and, in the process, others. I am trying to learn at this late date how to be good to myself, with full belief that goodness to others will more easily follow.

The tragic note is that it took loss of life to bring about the Death Row situation and the quest for self-understanding and improvement. Nothing I learn will cancel out that loss or relieve the suffering of loved ones left behind. Yet tragic as that is, it would be even more tragic if those lives were lost and nothing was learned from the bitter lessons they taught.

These lessons have not been learned easily or without constant effort. Many times in the past I have been dissatisfied with my life, but there was no real assistance available in the prisons. Each time I read books describing methods for understanding and changing character, personality, or conduct, some supernatural intervention was required; i.e., do such and such and "somehow" you would reap beneficial results or "someone" would give you the strength or "God will give you the answer." Never having felt myself worthy of supernatural intervention, I became skeptical of such writings. Years passed and my conduct repeated itself though I remained dissatisfied with my life. I ended up here on Death Row.

Then in late 1965, after more than a year on Death Row, I finally learned an effective way to change myself by myself.

Dr. Maxwell Maltz, in his book *Psycho-Cybernetics,* articulates many psychological principles by which personality and behavior changes can be made by any individual—without professional or divine assistance.

After I studied the book thoroughly, trying to disprove the principles with my cultivated skepticism, I became convinced of its effectiveness. I might add that the principles of the book have recently been confirmed for me by a highly competent psychologist.

Human personality and behavior are determined by past experience stored in the memory bank of our brain. A mass of scientific evidence establishes that this memory bank is in the subconscious mind and that the human brain and nervous system perform together exactly like the now familiar electronic computer. They are servo-mechanisms, goal-striving guidance systems controlled by the conscious mind. They operate on stored experience (information), whether it is success- or failure-oriented.

The most important discovery was that which established the inability of the subconscious mind to distinguish between an "actual" experience and an experience "vividly imagined in detail." Both clinical and experimental psychologists have proved this fact.

These discoveries make it possible for anyone to synthesize "experience" and act as his own programmer to bring about personality and character changes. The idea is to supplant "actual" undesirable past experiences with more desirable "imaginary" experiences. The subconscious mind, unable to distinguish between these kinds of experience, will then operate automatically on this newly stored "experience" just as if it were real, and the person will behave in a way consistent with his new self-image. In effect, the imaginary desirable image becomes the subconscious you, and the subconscious determines the greater part of all human conduct.

Of course these changes do not occur overnight. An essential of the program is repetition: imagining the desirable course of conduct or personality trait vividly and in detail, seeing yourself actually "living" the new role. This must be done diligently for thirty minutes each day for no less than twenty-one days. I have maintained such a schedule for a number of years now and found it to be effective.

I have given an extremely sketchy outline, but I believe the principles can be easily demonstrated to anyone willing to try them, skeptics included. Even skeptics would find it hard to dispute the obvious fact that we learn to function successfully by experiencing success, and so long as experience can be synthesized we can each be successful as human beings. The principles are grounded in the well-recognized area of self-image psychology.

For me, the idea that the subconscious mind could not distinguish between an actual and an imaginary experience, and that I no longer needed to rely on supernatural intervention or pure will power to alter my behavior, was the most amazing information I had ever received. It meant that I could be anything I wanted to be within my physical capabilities; I could act any way I wanted to act. Nothing limited me except my own imagination. Past history need not influence me. Psycho-cybernetics permitted me to escape at last from the experiences of my past.

With this new information and a great deal of enthusiasm, I established a program for myself.

I compiled a list of every illegal act I could remember committing. Then I began studying elementary books about "growing up" and "what it means to grow up," which helped determine desirable character traits, behavior patterns, methods for solving moral problems and, in general, clean living habits. I next completed some self-analysis motivational tests to determine what had generally motivated my past conduct. From the outcome of these efforts I arranged a "hierarchy of values" that would permit me to function in society with a minimum of harm to others and a maximum of benefits for myself. A principle of general semantics is that contentment and intelligent, harmonious living are designed into the very structure of every human being. I want to function in just such a manner.

Once I had determined the type of conduct and principles that would best allow me to function within the above minimum and maximum limitations, I began a program of "re-experiencing" each of the illegal acts on my previously compiled list—only this time behaving within the newly selected patterns, so that the illegal act was not repeated. It was very time-consuming. After having re-experienced past illegal conduct I began imagining a wide variety of situations in which I would likely find myself if ever I were again released into society. In each of these additional "experiences" only the new values were ever involved, the past ones having been totally eliminated from my mind during these sessions. I deliberately contrived many temptations in these imaginary experiences and "lived" the incident as vividly as possible. The experience was reinforced by "feeling" the elation of resisting each temptation. I further envisioned myself in many situations where I could solve moral problems that would seriously affect either myself or another person. The newly selected values were called upon and the least amount of harm possible was done. Further, I employed psycho-cybernetics to learn how to be more open with and concerned for other people, an essential ability for adjusting to a complex society.

Now, after seven years on Death Row, and notwithstanding previous psychiatric and psychologic opinion to the contrary, I do not doubt my ability to set and work toward long-term goals. I do not doubt my ability to adjust to society. And I do not doubt that I have overcome the influences of past conduct.

My personal accomplishments on Death Row are partial but satisfying, even if I must take them to the deadly gas chamber. But how much more could be accomplished by me and other men on other death rows across the country if you, society, would decide that salvaging human beings is as important as salvaging material things.

Everything in the universe, inevitably and unalterably, is in a state of constant change. Why must a condemned man be trapped impossibly in a static nature based on a past event registered in words in a court record? It would be to society's advantage to help men like me direct this change and thereby return to society a useful human being. When that time arrives there will be more justification for calling this an enlightened society.

James W. L. Park

JAMES W. L. PARK is associate warden for San Quentin prison, a professional penologist with many years in the California penal system. He, more than any other man, represents authority to the ninety-five men presently condemned to death in California. It is he who authorizes visits and correspondence for the men on Death Row. He has helped the progress of this book greatly by allowing numerous "special purpose" visits with the six contributors who come under his jurisdiction. He is held in various levels of esteem by the men on Death Row.

But it is not easy to be an administrator of Death Row. It is not a simple thing to be the keeper of men's lives, their captor. I have spoken with several guards, associate wardens and wardens, the only men who go voluntarily to prison. Each has indicated that he had to choose his own way of dealing with the stresses that confining other men imposes on the mind. It is often difficult to tell the captives from the captors; often they appear to be in an almost sibling rivalry. An interdependency develops; each depends on the other to do "easy time."

A few months ago, while speaking with an individual in authority at another California prison, a man responsible for the lives of thousands of inmates, a man of compassion and a considerable degree of objectivity, I was told, "You have to take what they (the inmates) say and what we (the prison administrators) say and find the truth somewhere in between." He had worked it out, come to understand something of his relationship to himself and to the men for whom he felt responsible; but he said it had been very difficult for the first few years. As a guard at Folsom, many years before, the element of competition and violence had been so upsetting that he came to hate his job and many convicts. He told me he used to lull himself to sleep by imagining bringing certain prisoners into the Big Yard and machine-gunning them. It took him a long time to come to terms with himself. In many respects his growth is not unlike the growth of the condemned writers who comprise this book.

Park is considered by his peers the intellectual of the department. He is the spokesman for the whole prison as well, the man most often quoted in newspaper articles referring to San Quentin. He is the voice of authority in many ways. It would be gratifying if there were no need for a man of his talents, if there were no such job to be filled. It would be best for all involved, Park as well, if he were vice president of a large life insurance firm instead of executor for Death Row.

"Now it is a terrible business to mark out a man for the vengeance of men. But it is a thing to which a man can grow accustomed .... And the horrible thing about public officials, even the best ... is not that they are wicked ... not that they are stupid ... it is simply that they have got used to it."

G.K. Chesterton

An Interview with James Park

Approaching San Quentin prison. Sunny March seventeenth, 1971. St. Patrick's Day.
Going for a visit to the Death Clinic, for an interview with Associate Warden James Park . . . .

L: You mentioned receiving the book by Jack Rainsberger that we published. Thought I would bring along this other book we did as well. It's a basic Buddhist mindfulness exercise given monks upon entering the monastery. I would like to send several to the prison library if I may. It's a useful tool, very calming. I guess if an inmate could see this place as a monastery, as a very few I have met do, he could use some of his enforced time very productively. He might find more of himself than he originally presumed.

P: Well, we have had a yoga group going here which I presume has a similar effect, certainly about turning inward and meditating and expanding consciousness and so forth.

Yeah, if more people were sitting around and meditating we wouldn't have so many people killing each other, or trying to kill each other.

L: There's a great deal of violence now?

P: Well, you've got to qualify that. We've had thirteen stabbings in the last week. But what we're talking about involves two percent of the population, you know, like anywhere else.

L: Is this racial?

P: It is now, yeah . . . .

L: It wasn't in the beginning?

P: No.

L: What kicked it off?

P: Well, the initial thing was a private matter—I don't know whether it was a debt or some kind of disagreement. It started a week ago Monday night, when a black was cut by a chicano. On Tuesday morning two whites were cut, apparently by two blacks—again this was a private matter, some kind of shenanigans they were up to. But from that point apparently some of the youngsters who were real hostile people decided to retaliate and make it a racial thing. It didn't start that way.

L: You say "youngsters"; what do you mean?

P: Relative youngsters—I'm talking about men twenty-two, twenty-three, twenty-four.

L: Are there the same hassles in Folsom where they don't allow people under twenty-five? I understand many inmates feel Folsom is an elite place to be.

P: They have less trouble. It's just like many prisoners would prefer here to Soledad. Number one, the average age is a little bit older. You see, much of Soledad's trouble reflects age more than anything else because the younger prisoners, as might be expected, jump around more; they get into more hassles; they'll flash into a spontaneously violent situation or similar situation very quickly. At Folsom everything's kind of set and predictable and you know where you stand. And because the age is considerably older than at Soledad, people aren't jumping around as fast.

L: You don't think that the presence of a death row in this prison as opposed to any of the other prisons in California has any deterrent effect on violence?

P: I don't think it has any effect at all. Death Row is apart. Our people are just as isolated from Death Row, by and large, as people out in the outside community.

L: Some people believe capital punishment is a deterrent but if killings are occurring right next door to the gas chamber, it doesn't seem to mean a thing.

P: We really can't prove it one way or the other. It certainly isn't a massive deterrent because there isn't that much difference between states that have it and states that don't. If it was really holding down an awful lot of murders, then there'd be a big difference. I would think it probably holds down a few murders maybe, but probably a negligible amount.

L: Dovie Mathis mentioned to me in a letter that ten of the men on the Row had put together a manuscript called "Reflections of the Condemned" for use by a teacher at the College of San Mateo. I asked him if I could see it in hopes that some of the work might be included in the book we're working on. But he mentioned that some of the inmates that were on Death Row then are gone now and that he could not contact them for permissions to use their works. Now, where would they have gone?

P: Oh, a lot of them are gone. . . . You see, in the last eight years we've had over a hundred new trials granted. The Supreme Court of California and the U.S. Supreme Court overturned the death verdicts in that many cases. Some of them come back with another death penalty. In fact, some will come back with a death penalty for the fourth time now, which means to say they originally had a guilt trial and then a penalty phase trial when they were sentenced to death. One man has had, since his original trial, three more penalty trials, and each time he draws a jury that sentences him to death. Other men get life on their second or third time around, and go into a general prison population somewhere. Of course, some of them have had their sentences commuted by governors in the past. Some have had their sentences reduced arbitrarily by the California Supreme Court. They looked at the case and said, well, this isn't anything more than second-degree murder, and they reduced the sentence down. This happened in at least two cases—much to the disgust of the men involved, because if they stayed under sentence of death, they would get very quick access clear up to the U.S. Supreme Court; but when you're a prisoner just serving time, the courts grind very, very slowly.

It might take them years to get to the same place they could get to in months from Death Row. Of course, it's a chance again, because as a mainline prisoner, you know all you're losing is time. But if you're on Death Row, you may lose your life, if you fool around with it too long. But for right now we're in sort of a lull, because we're waiting, and the inmates are waiting, for the U.S. Supreme Court to get off its duff and make a decision on two major cases before them that might change the whole trial thing all around.*

L: I've heard they'll make the decision this week?

P: Well, I heard it was going to be made this week three months ago too, so I don't know. I hope so, because we're up to about ninety-three men here on Death Row and we don't have much more room. We're sort of running out of space.

L: What happens if the Supreme Court upholds the trial procedure as being in keeping with their interpretation of the Constitution? Would that open the way for executions again? Would that end the nearly four-year moratorium?

P: Again, that depends on the courts. The procedure, and what has happened in the last eight years, is that a man gets a death date and files an appeal to the U.S. Supreme Court, having gone through all the other motions that you have to go through, and almost invariably the U. S. Supreme Court issues a stay of execution and considers the case. The real key is going to be not so much what they decide in these cases, but what their whole general attitude is going to be. If they continue to be as free in granting stays and considering these appeals as they have been in the last few years, then I don't think we'll see many executions. If they take a position like they did

---

*On 3 May 1971 the Supreme Court decided 6-3 that a man found guilty of a capital offense is not due a separate "penalty" trial to tell his side of the story before a penalty is handed down, though the Fifth Amendment of the Constitution declares that he need not incriminate himself. The Court also ruled that a jury need not be given guidelines as to how the law applies to handing down a sentence of death (though guidelines are provided for the lesser sentence of confinement), thereby giving the power of life or death to the jury without due instruction as to the pertinence of the death penalty under specific circumstances. These two rulings cut the throats of some five hundred of the more than six hundred beings awaiting some compassion from the courts.

on haircuts in schools and don't want to mess with it, and they send these things back and decline to hear them, then I would suspect we would get close to some executions. But it's still a long way away; we're not about to have a mass execution scene.

L: There hasn't been an execution here in three years? Four years?

P: Four years. April twelfth, 1967. Aaron Mitchell from Sacramento.

L: Have you ever seen an execution?

P: Yes. Saw Mitchell.

L: How did it affect you afterwards?

P: Well . . . it seemed like a terribly irrevocable act. You know, it's the kind of social decision that you can't recall, modify, change, or rectify. This is my primary reaction to the thing.

L: Do you think it should be abolished?

P: Oh, I don't take a particularly strong stand on it . . . . I'm not a fan of capital punishment. I'm sort of against people killing people just in general. I think willful killing of people is not right. But I'm always bothered, maybe because I am a Libra and always have to weigh everything, you know. Maybe it's a bad act to kill these men, yet, what they did, many of them, were very bad scenes also.

L: You mentioned to me in previous conversations that several men are still quite violent.

P: The records do show that there have been assaults between prisoners. But some men get passive . . . . You get in this dilemma. I think historically it is borne out that the majority of men on Death Row will probably not kill again; they will not be a hazard again. Yet some, some will. I don't take a big crusading stand in this thing. I think it's up to the community; they've got to decide what they want. My particular philosophy, sort of, is if the community feels very strongly that it needs something even if it's wrong, then I guess it deserves to have it. Otherwise you get into the elitism bag and say what's good for people. But again, if you look at the long historical thing, like six thousand years, societies have always taken steps to protect themselves, or to do what they think protects themselves, and I think this is not a thing you wipe out by passing a law. You don't wipe out this apparently deep-seated need for vengeance which, I think, lies in all of us. It certainly lies in society. It's certainly one of the predominant social emotions at the time that a murder is committed—particularly an atrocious murder; and it's equally strong at the time when the murderer is convicted.

L: How long a time is there now between conviction and execution? Four years? Five years?

P: Yes. Well, by the time a man gets to be executed, the feeling of vengeance has pretty much dropped out.

L: Although with Chessman, the feelings of vengeance grew as the time between his sentencing and execution became longer and longer.

P: Well, yeah, there was a lot of very strong feeling on both sides about Chessman. I wasn't directly connected with the situation. I was of the opinion that Chessman sort of outsmarted himself. If he hadn't really turned on such a tremendous public controversy about himself, the governor might well have quietly commuted him.* But once he got out there as a "cause celebre," he became a measuring point: you know, you're for or against him; you're for sin or against it. I think that probably put the governor in an impossible position, in terms of how he could act.

L: You mentioned once that Chessman's egocentricity was such that some officials in a sort of black jest used to say that if he had been executed on a Friday, he would have arisen on a Sunday. Were there a lot of people who felt that kind of dislike for him?

P: Well, I haven't made a big research on this, but I know that many people that knew him and dealt with him indicated this arrogance was very strong in his personality.

L: Was he less violent after he started writing?

P: I'm not sure about that.

---

* A prominent Los Angeles attorney, when asked if one of his condemned clients could be included in this book, declined on the grounds that bringing attention to a case might only make the prosecution more ambitious.

L: In his books he mentions that he tried to keep out of beefs.

P: Well, on Death Row, it's a little bit harder to get into beefs than it is elsewhere.

L: Isn't there a point where everybody locks out together?

P: Yes.

L: And that's where all the troubles happen, right? It can't happen otherwise?

P: This is pretty well true.

L: Nobody's ever been found beaten up in his cell?

P: No. But another factor too, whether writing a book has anything to do with it or not, he was also getting older; and our experience is much like the auto insurance experience that people over twenty-five are less risky in terms of jumping around and getting into daily hassles than people under twenty-five. So Chessman was older and it's an interesting thing... my observation of Death Row, even though it is an extremely limited situation in terms of your sphere of operation, is that many men have become better men there, more controlled, maybe less prone to interfere with the rights of other people.

L: Do you think that affects the governor's or the court's decision? I mean, what's happened after the crime.

P: Well, it would have to affect the governor's decision because he has to take into account everything that happens, and this is one reason why I try to be very careful not to discuss men on the Row as personalities, whether they're mean and ornery or real good, and this sort of thing.

L: There's a lot of creativity on Death Row right now, isn't there?

P: Well, yes, but.... I make a point that this becomes remarkable and you notice it because you really hadn't expected that this would come off of Death Row. I don't have any doubt that there is creativity up there because again, the men on Death Row, by and large, aren't any better or any worse than the men in the prison in general, who in turn reflect their particular socio-economic class outside. So there is creativity.

L: Is there much cooperation amongst the men who are

writing on the Row? Dovie has been working with three other men on this book as "inside editor" with what seems to be considerable cooperation and communication.

P: Well, they get along in small groups.... Here in the prison thing, in the prison setting generally, it's like the man said, "everybody's an island." It's particularly true with the kind of people we have that they interact at certain points and for certain reasons, but their ability to fully trust each other is limited. Here again, this is not too different from people out-side as a whole.

L: Are most of the men on Death Row family men? Since the majority of murders occur within the family.

P: No, very few, very few. This is one progress I think this state has made; by and large, wife-killers and people who killed in family squabbles don't get to the Row. We don't have very many there: two or three, four, something like that. And in one case it was a pretty well planned-out conspiracy. Well thought out. But, by and large, your people who kill their wives don't get the death penalty. They come to prison, do about ten years and then go out and you never see them again.

L: Getting back to what is of such great concern to so many people at this time: if the decision of the U.S. Supreme Court should go against the appeals presently before it, will there be executions this year?

P: Well, there won't be a blood-bath, if that's what you mean. We aren't going to line them up outside the gas cham-ber door and make them wait their turns.

L: What will happen in that case?

P: Oh, there might be six or eight executions but I doubt if there will be any more than that.*

---

* In June, just as this book was being finished, Associate Warden Park told me: "It looks like now we are going to have Death Row Three; next year this time we might have one hundred twenty men on the Row. But I doubt there will be any executions before spring 1972."

Robert Massie

ROBERT MASSIE, A-90159, Death Row, San Quentin, California, is a pale, sensitive, quiet-spoken Virginian of twenty-nine years who demands his execution. He claims that to keep him alive and pinned to the collection board of the condemned is in violation of the Constitution and is "cruel and unusual punishment." (Ironically, before the Supreme Court now is the question as to whether execution itself is not indeed in violation of that same Eighth Amendment.) He feels he can't win either way. He recognizes and deeply regrets the taking of another human being's life. He wishes either to be immediately put to death or to be immediately set free. In either case he wishes to start anew, to begin again, to continue in the growth that this present life may afford or, if necessary, to start again in another moment of birth. Through an extensive abuse of drugs, and "speed" in particular, he found himself the slayer. He wants out.

As he wrote in a letter: "All action starts in, and is a result of, consciousness; but to be conscious of my present surroundings is akin to suffering the torments of total despair with no hope of respite, and bordering on the nightmare world of insanity."

Robert Massie is one of those condemned who has very few visitors and little correspondence with the outside world. He is one of those lonely men for whom time is a great burden; for whom meditation is life; for whom the separation from life is death. It took him three years to "awake from the lethargy of prolonged drug use." He awoke to Vedanta and the teachings of Vivekananda: "I suddenly wanted to know the purpose of my existence, who and what I was as a conscious entity." He has had four dates for execution, the last of which came within thirty-six hours of being carried out. "When they came and told me I was not to be executed, I was disappointed, angry."

When we met our conversation was of Vivekananda and god-visioned Ramakrishna. He said, "If I was out of here tomorrow, I'd head for a yoga ashram and stay there for six months to get really clear. Then you and I could sit down on the beach and really get into some writing and living."

Having published in *Esquire* and *Teen,* Massie is considered the only professional writer on the Row at San Quentin now. (His newest work is entitled *Prisons: Scourge of the Nation.*) He is not one to misuse words or emotions; he was direct and to the point when he told me, with eyes averted to the concrete floor of the room in which we met, "You know my feelings; it would be just fine by me if I went out of here tomorrow in a redwood box. If they aren't going to allow me to be free, they might as well kill me and get it done with."

Death by Degrees

Robert Massie

"It is the judgment of this court that you be delivered to the Warden of the State Prison at San Quentin, California, to be by him put to death in the manner provided by law." These were the ominous words which assailed my ears in May, 1965. Since that time I have been given four dates on which to die: October 10, 1967, November 2, 1967, November 15, 1967, and March 12, 1969. Each time I mentally prepared myself to accept what seemed to be the inevitable: made a list of the food I preferred for the traditional last meal, chose the institutional chaplain who was to preside as my spiritual adviser, and made a will for the disposition of my personal possessions. After completing these formalities, all that was left for me to do was to steel myself to make the trip to the gas chamber with all the dignity I was capable of mustering. Each time I did, this death was averted by judicial or executive action. You who are reading this are probably thinking that I have been extremely lucky or that I am a highly skilled neophyte-attorney who has manipulated the courts into granting stays of execution. Nothing could be further from the truth.

I, Robert L. Massie (Prison No. A-90159), have been sentenced to die for my complicity in causing a person's death during what was called an attempted robbery. The circumstances surrounding my conviction and death sentence are unimportant to the purpose of this narrative.

For the past five and a half years I have been confined to a four-by-ten-foot cell on Death Row and have handled my own defense on appeal, as the law allows. . . .

Why have the various courts continuously stopped my execution? The official reason for these interventions has been: "pending the outcome of the issues that are now before us." What issues? That there are no standardized guidelines for *juries* that sentence a man to death. Well, I find no fault and have no quarrel with this contention and believe it should be resolved before taking the life of anyone. But I pled guilty to first-degree murder and was tried by a judge, not a jury. Therefore I fail to see how my case warrants consideration within the context of this argument. Even if there is a remote possibility that my case is deserving of this extrajudicial review, I have advised this Court that I am satisfied with the mandate of California and to restore my date of execution *forthwith.* But as stated above, petitioning the courts for my legal rights has been completely unavailing.

If the reason for these delays is because the courts are genuinely concerned about my sanity and/or incompetency, notwithstanding the fact that the psychiatric staff at San Quentin has already examined me and declared me to be competent and sane, then why have I not been brought before the courts for a hearing to determine this so-called question? The law states that if I am insane the proceedings against me cannot continue; that I must be removed to a medical facility for psychiatric care. If there is any merit to these contentions, why have I been forced to remain on Death Row all these years without psychiatric treatment? Obviously, the continued stays of my judgment are nothing but ploys and legal subterfuge, employed to further the ends of unsolicited counsel. They could not care less about my sanity and general well-being.

Before I proceed further, I think it appropriate to state unequivocally that I am not an advocate of capital punishment. The death penalty serves no purpose other than to prove that the states which retain it have progressed no further in moral values than the individuals they kill in the name of the law. This law has no place in a Christian country; it never has had. Anyone who professes to be a Christian is saying that he is a "follower of Christ." My questions to the Christians are:

Would Christ order my death? Would he condemn me to a four-by-ten cell year after year, giving me dates of execution, and bringing me back from the brink of death each time the sentence was about to be executed? Would He subject me to this kind of mental torment? Since we all know He would not participate in these atrocities, then how are Christians able to justify the laws which permit such inhumanity to man? If you are adherents to the Mosaic law, which advocates "an eye for an eye and a tooth for a tooth," then my question is: Would Moses subject me to years of mental torment before putting me to death? I did not confine my victim for years in prison under the constant threat of death before killing him, so why is it being done unto me? Moreover, if the law of Moses is considered the proper remedy for dealing with violators of manmade law, then the coming of Christ and His teachings are meaningless and should be deleted from our Bibles.

Most of the zeal which prosecutors display in their efforts to get a man condemned to death is to further their political ambitions rather than to see that justice is served. As long as there remains an elective system for placing prosecutors in office, justice will remain secondary to political aspiration. Since this office is a stepping stone to political advancement by building up a successful record of convictions, instead of a reputation for honesty and integrity, citizens of low income will seldom receive fair trials.

Notwithstanding my feelings about the death penalty, and contrary to the views of most of the other condemned men, I much prefer that my valid judgment (which I am not protesting) be speedily executed in accordance with the now existing law of California. Having my sentence reduced to life in prison would be a fate much worse than death.

Actually, it is only fitting that my life should culminate in the gas chamber. From the time I was seven years old I have been a ward of the state. From the years of seven to ten I was placed in a number of foster homes; from eleven to fourteen I lived in the state reformatory (euphemistically called a "training school for boys"); and from fifteen to twenty-three, I was in jails and penitentiaries. Finally, at the age of twenty-three I was delivered to the warden at San Quentin, where it is hoped that I will shortly graduate to the merciful oblivion called *death*. It is readily apparent that my years of penal servitude have not helped me, nor has it helped society. Therefore, what would be gained by spending the rest of my natural life in prison? I have never contributed anything worthwhile to society and never will.

For what reason should I strive to have my judgment of death reduced to life in prison? Is life on earth such a blessing or so precious that I should be desirous of spending it in a dehumanized hellhole of steel and concrete where the law of the jungle and degeneracy reign supreme, where all human and moral values are considered a weakness? Am I insane because I would prefer going on to what may be a better sphere of life, the after-death region? Rotting away in prison for the rest of my days and deteriorating mentally, perhaps even going completely insane, is not a very pleasing incentive for continuing to cling to this life. Besides, I agree with the words of Mohandas K. Gandhi, who said: "Both birth and death are great mysteries. If death is not a prelude to another life, the intermediate period is a cruel mockery." Therefore, the state will actually be doing me a favor by prematurely ending my miserable earthly sojourn.

Death is the king of terror, the "grim reaper" whom all mortals are one day destined to meet. Perhaps Death has been mislabeled and in truth is a benign old gentleman who beckons us to a richer and fuller life, leaving all our sorrows and strife behind. Whatever his disposition, it is certainty that we shall all travel to his domain, and there is no power on earth which will prevent it. So why should Death be feared?

I, a conscious entity, do not remember having any fear of becoming a resident in this mortal body at birth, so it is unreasonable to cringe in terror when the time arrives for my departure from this vehicle of flesh. What is so frightening about returning to my native abode, the plane of consciousness where I dwelled before I began this mortal journey? Dying is not unusual. People do it every day. And a few whiffs of the lethal substance called cyanide is probably no more painful than being burned to death in an auto collision, a policeman's bullet, or a host of other death-dealing agents.

For those who may be wondering why I do not attempt to commit suicide, since I seem to be in such a rush to get it over with, let me say that my beliefs in a deity expressly forbid me to commit this act. Furthermore, I do not want to deprive the state of doing its own dirty work. If I had my way about it, I would make them televise my execution. Since the state sees fit to sanction the death penalty, I think it is only fair that the taxpayers get their money's worth and be permitted to observe this ritualistic ceremony. Why is a legal murder conducted behind closed doors? What about the alleged deterrent value that capital punishment is supposed to have on the John Doe citizen who might be tempted to commit an act which would warrant his suffering the death penalty? Morbid scenes involving intricate plots for murder are shown on the television screen every day. What would be so unusual about televising an execution? Would this not make the death penalty a much more effective deterrent?

I have grown bitter. I have become contemptuous of American law and its brand of justice. I have come to despise those persons responsible for the violation of my human and legal rights. I seek justice as did the People, who declared that I must die. Justice demands an answer to the question: "When?" Those persons proclaiming to uphold and mete out justice have been not only blind but mute, deaf and insensitive. Every critic of our courts, whom I now join, has stressed that punishment must be swift if it is to serve any valid purpose. I stand as a living testimonial to the excruciating, deliberately contrived slowness with which the courts have applied justice for the People, making me more a victim than the person whose death I caused.

Suppose a person, after conditioning himself to meet this fate with a degree of equanimity, is told just thirty-six hours (the amount of time I had left to live) prior to the event that he has been given a stay of execution. According to popular belief this individual would be extremely elated and would profusely thank his oppressors for sparing him for a few more months of life in a dingy prison cell. I can state categorically that this was not my reaction or state of mind when I was told for the fourth time that they had decided to prolong my miserable existence. I was disgusted. In my opinion this is cruel and unusual punishment in that it constitutes extreme mental torture and is a most flagrant violation of Article VIII of the Constitution of the United States. Why should the law be permitted to play with my life like a yo-yo by subjecting me to continuous dates of execution? Knowing that I am going to die, why should I be made to suffer further years of confinement? The law is clear, and I have every right to demand immediate execution.

End & Beginning

From a very early age, I was left to my own devices and, consequently, no real moral values were made a part of my education. As a teenager I was restless, with no thought of the future. I had no goals beyond searching for daily, excitement. My quest for excitement was actually a means to escape from the ordinary responsibilities of life and to avoid having to conform to the mundane ideas of the masses.

With no perspective and no regard for the rights of others, I began committing petty crimes which eventually caused my commitment to prison at the ripe old age of fifteen. In prison my attitude toward life remained unchanged and my general outlook became warped and distorted. With my limited ability to cope with everyday conflicts and the anxieties produced by a prison atmosphere, I resorted to the use of drugs, which were smuggled into the penitentiary from unknown sources. For a while my mental horizons seemed to expand and I spent my time devising schemes for undermining all of the lawful authority which I so bitterly resented. It was not long before most of my concepts of right and wrong were completely obliterated from consciousness, and in their place "do what thou wilt" became the permanent code to which I adhered. The use of drugs (mostly amphetamine, "speed") crippled my will power and destroyed my power of concentration. Symptoms of paranoia were immediately obvious to everyone with whom I came in contact, and I subsequently became a menace to everyone, including myself.

From "Recollections from Death Row," *Teen* magazine, January 1971. Reprinted with permission of *Teen* magazine.

Upon my release from prison, I continued the use of drugs because they had become a way of life, a psychological crutch. I lived in a world of fantasy, and anyone who threatened to intrude or destroy my world of illusions became a potential enemy. Because of my psychotic state of mind and the petty crimes committed for daily sustenance, I was returned to prison for further education. Needless to say, my second stretch in prison was no more conducive to rehabilitation than the first. I became more withdrawn and my hatred of society became so intense that I was unable to formulate any meaningful or intelligent plans for the future. After a while my only thoughts were of how I could maintain a continuous supply of drugs, which would enable me to exist indefinitely in the rosy world of illusion. Nothing else mattered. In this frame of mind, I was again returned to free society.

Because of my mental instability I drifted from one place to another. My years of confinement from a very early age and the use of dangerous drugs combined to make me incapable of coping with the standards of free society. Friendless, without guidance, I became frustrated. Without references I was unable to obtain decent employment, so I staged several armed robberies and caused a person's death during one of these unlawful acts. For this death I was sentenced by the court to die.

After I had been on Death Row for approximately three years, I began waking from the lethargic aftermath of the prolonged use of drugs. I suddenly wanted to know the purpose of my existence, who and what I was as a conscious entity. The partial answers to this self-questioning began to slowly filter through my brain. I realized the tragic waste I had made of my life and concluded that the belated inner stirrings toward self-improvement and further education had come too late. I wondered if my destiny had been preordained and about my future prospects if my death sentence were reduced to life in prison. Delving into various philosophies increased my insight and made me even more aware of the beauties of life and the destructive path I had followed . . . .

Why do some people succeed in leading useful lives while others fail? There are numerous answers to this question, and each of us must look within himself for the applicable answer. In my case, the drug which is commonly referred to as "speed" was the predominant factor in bringing about my complete destruction. In the beginning speed produced a state of euphoria, an inner sense of well-being, which caused me to think that I had made a most wonderful discovery. I became keenly sensitive to my surroundings, as well as to the people around me, and I was riding "high" for weeks at a time. Eventually I became psychologically and physically addicted. Subtle changes in personality began to occur and were perceptible to everyone but me. I soon reached the point where I ceased to experience the pleasant high that resulted in the beginning stages. My tolerance level became so great that I was eventually mainlining (injecting intravenously) three and four tubes of Wyamine every day for as long as five or six days in succession; thereafter taking two or three days to recuperate before beginning another trip for the same length of time. (Wyamine is a nose inhaler with a piece of cotton inside, containing mephentermine.) Resorting to the use of Wyamine was not a matter of choice. For some reason the undercover connection who had been smuggling drugs into prison was no longer able to supply the demand for Benzedrine and the other forms of speed. After two and a half years of that routine, I became submerged in a nightmare world, completely disoriented and totally alienated from most of my fellow humans. My powers of concentration became so limited that I was unable to remember most things from one minute to the next. Believe it or not, I am still feeling the aftereffects of this drug, though I have not used it for six years.

Although the *final* reckoning is yet to come, the devastating effect of words is ever present. For the remainder of my life I must bear the odious brands—"killer" and "murderer." What are mere words? What image do you call forth when those two words are applied to another human being? Yes, I know. You call forth the common, dehumanized image.

The men residing on Death Row have been pictured either as a bunch of snarling animals or as something less than human. Citizens of free society seldom visit Death Row. However, on one occasion when the associate warden accompanied some visitors to our domain, I distinctly overheard one visitor say, "This isn't what I expected. These men appear to be like everyone else." I suppose he had mentally envisioned Death Row as some kind of zoo where a lot of subhumans would attempt to lunge out and bite him. Some of the other visitors appeared to be wide-eyed with amazement, and it was readily apparent that they had entertained similar ideas. It must have been very disconcerting to see us engaged in the normal activities of playing cards, watching television, reading, and having friendly discussions among ourselves. Several of us extended them a cordial greeting and this seemed to relax their clearly discernible facial tension. If one of us had said "boo," quite possibly one of the elderly amongst these visitors would have suffered a heart attack.

Living on Death Row year after year causes a great deal of mental strain, and it often requires a tremendous effort to control our anxieties. Nevertheless, most of the men are very successful at maintaining congenial relations with the guards. There are occasional outbursts of pent-up tension, but this has become a rarity. The majority are endeavoring to learn all they can about the law, which will render them more capable of assisting the attorneys who are handling their cases.

Although the men on Death Row are considered outcasts from society, a number of them who have labored under these conditions for four or five years, reflecting on their misspent lives, could be safely returned to free society as useful members. That statement might sound absurd, but some of the men who came within a few days of making the transition called death have undergone psychological transformation. Their attitudes and conduct no longer appear hostile or antisocial. I believe it is fairly well known that when a man faces a life-and-death crisis, his dormant strength of character and the best of his latent qualities can be brought to the surface. If the light of realization dawns on his conscious mind, the negative and destructive attitudes which brought him to this station in life gradually diminish, and in their place comes the desire for truth and further education. Unfortunately, this renovation of thinking will come too late for most of us. The time is swiftly approaching for a decision from the U. S. Supreme Court which will undoubtedly herald the rescheduling of our dates with the executioner, and I believe many will die. Although I am not lamenting my fate, I would sincerely like to see most if not all of these men given a chance to redeem themselves. Contrary to the contentions of the prosecutors, many of the crimes which brought them here were unpremeditated and no more merited the imposition of the death penalty than the men walking the prison yard who were convicted of similar or worse crimes.

Because of the turmoil currently existing within the United States (bombings, civil disobedience, etc.), it is very unlikely that the death penalty will be abolished in the very near future. Therefore, the men like myself, who have been on Death Row for a number of years and have exhausted most of the legal avenues which will prolong their existence, will probably be leaving this world by the middle of this next year, maybe sooner. The next date I receive for execution will be my fifth, and though I have long been inured and mentally prepared to face this lethal ceremony with a degree of equanimity, I cannot help but wonder about the exact day on which life will end.

*   *   *

Dear Stephen:

About the only information I can add to what I've already written about the use of drugs is that men in prison who are sensitive and ill equipped to cope with the harsh realities of this environment of hate, cruelty, and perversity in every form, an environment totally devoid of love and compassion, generally resort to the use of drugs to blot out the horrors of man's inhumanity to man and to retain a measure of sanity. Otherwise, the continual subjection to penal oppression without any

137

form of relief would drive some of these men insane, and others to commit suicide. Therefore, it is very difficult to determine the lesser of the two evils.

The loneliness of our incarceration in a rigidly controlled environment is beyond the average citizen's comprehension. Years of isolation from all normal activities without a moment of respite has a harrowing effect on the human spirit. The majority of these men are literally starved for love and affection, but they will NEVER find it in this place unless people outside begin to recognize their obligations and take steps to reform these decadent, soul-destroying institutions. Just a little contact with others—an occasional letter, etc.—would be a tremendous boon to the development of healthier attitudes, and in no time at all these men would be responding to their better instincts. However, they are without the resources for locating the type of people who would be willing to respond to these needs, and must therefore continue to endure more long years of anguish, loneliness and despair.

Edgar Smith

EDGAR SMITH, No. 34837, Death Row, New Jersey State Prison, Trenton, New Jersey, has been on Death Row longer than any other man in American history. He was illegally convicted in 1957 of the killing of a fifteen-year-old girl. (On 14 May 1971 the United States Court of Appeals reversed that conviction and ordered his release or a new trial.) An unsigned, coerced confession was the basis for his fourteen-year incarceration on Death Row. In those years he has grown from a twenty-three-year-old high school drop-out and ex-marine regarded as a drifter to a writer of two best-selling books *(Brief Against Death* and *A Reasonable Doubt)* and an accomplished "jailhouse lawyer" who has helped to prepare nineteen appeals on his own case as well as numerous appeals for fellow inmates.

When the Court of Appeals finally ruled on his case after Edgar Smith had been proclaiming his innocence for fourteen years, Judge Gibbons in a forty-two page opinion said that among a long series of faults in the prosecution of his case, Smith was never warned of his constitutional rights to remain silent, was not allowed to contact a lawyer, and was not properly brought before a magistrate for arraignment. The report of Judge Gibbons cites "Smith's gradual deterioration of spirit from cocky and confident at 11:30 p.m. on March 5, 1957 to subdued at 2:30 a.m. on March 6, to very restless and apprehensive and markedly agitated at 7:55 a.m., to broken and crying and finally trapped into an incriminating admission after 10:00 a.m." However, Smith insisted he would not sign the statement. "The purpose of the interrogation after 10:00 a.m.," stated Judge Gibbons in his overthrow of the unlawful conviction, "was not to determine who committed the crime but to obtain evidence of first degree murder."

Nevertheless, despite the questionable grounds for his conviction, twice Edgar Smith came within twenty-four hours of being executed. If he had not "grabbed hold" and educated himself in law he would not be alive today. He would not have stayed alive long enough to write the two best-selling books which netted him funds for his defense and caught the attention of William F. Buckley, Jr., who fought hard in his behalf and contacted top-rate lawyers. Had he remained the uneducated, rebellious, though equally innocent youth he was when accused, Edgar Smith would certainly have been put to death as so many others have been before him.

But the ambition and blindness of the State of New Jersey did not stop with Judge Gibbons overturning Smith's conviction. Robert Dilts, the Bergen County prosecutor, said after the reversal that it would be "extremely difficult" to bring Smith to trial again as was the state's option. But just minutes before he was to leave the Newark federal courthouse his bail was vacated and he was returned, tight-lipped, to the federal House of Detention, from which he was transferred to the state prison in Trenton. The inquisition has not ended and it may be some time before Edgar Smith is allowed freedom.

A Pre-posthumous Conversation with Myself

Edgar Smith

After fourteen years on Death Row, I'd like to say a few words about penal reform.

Q: Let's begin with your own situation. You have lived under a death sentence for fourteen years, considerably longer than the late Caryl Chessman. Do you think your execution at this late date would in any way benefit society, serve any useful purpose?

A: I'm not really certain any execution serves any useful purpose at any time, although I will agree it is probable that if you could induce mass amnesia, so that everyone alive would forget the crime of which I was convicted, there would still be some people—the head of the New Jersey Policemen's Benevolent Association, for one—who would think it a good thing, that something had been accomplished by my execution. Such people are obsessed with the notion that if you kill A, then B will not kill C.

Q: You don't believe in the deterrent theory, that punishment for one's crime will deter others from committing the same crime?

A: No, not really. Suppose they took me in the back room tomorrow and burned me—who would be deterred? Those who followed my trial back in 1957 but have long since forgotten it and me? The whole generation of teenagers who weren't even born at the time of my trial? I can't see it. The link between crime and punishment would be so remote, so tenuous, as to be effectively nonexistent.

Q: But the deterrent theory in general—what about that?

A: I cannot subscribe to it. The very people capital punishment is supposed to deter are the very people shielded from effective knowledge of what an execution is. Executions take place in antiseptic secrecy. The law says you cannot even publicize the day and time in advance, and that the general public may not witness the affair. All the public sees is a few lines in the morning newspaper saying so-and-so was executed at such-and-such a time. Those who do witness the execution—the curious prison guards, a few newsmen, perhaps a few spectacle-hungry police officers or public officials and their guests—are presumably not the people the execution is supposed to deter.

Q: Are you suggesting that executions be carried out in public?

A: I don't think there should be any executions until we see some proof that they accomplish something, but what the hell, if one believes in them, believes they deter people, then let's get them out in the open and deter lots of people. Let's stop acting ashamed of the fact that we are coldly and methodically killing people for no other reason than that we think, but cannot prove, that it does some good. Let's open up the execution chambers and show those we hope to deter just what is in store for them. After all, how much of a deterrent do you suppose nuclear weapons would be if they were nothing more to the Russians than a few lines in the morning newspapers?

Q: I don't know that I can accept that analogy, but let me ask you this. Douglas Lyons, a leader in a drive to abolish capital punishment, believes we should televise an execution, to show the public what it really is, what it is like. What do you think of that?

A: I would buy stock in the network doing the televising. It would get a better rating than the Super Bowl.

Q: But would it accomplish anything?

A: Sure it would. It would make the network a ton of money. They could get General Electric, or Dow Chemical, or perhaps the American Hoisting Company, to sponsor it—depending upon whether it was an electrocution, gassing, or hanging, and they could get Bert Parks to sing something appropriate as the guy walked to the chair. Groovy! And how about the instant replays and summer reruns?

Q: You don't take the suggestion seriously?

A: Not really, no more seriously than it is made. But if they ever did it in a culture as show-biz oriented and violent as ours, it would probably wind up a continuing series, at which point it would lose all meaning and be canceled for poor ratings. When Americans can turn on the TV at seven o'clock any weeknight and see their husbands and sons and brothers being killed in Vietnam, they aren't too likely to have a continuing interest in the execution of convicted murderers.

Q: How does an execution affect the other men on Death Row, those who have to watch the condemned men walk to their deaths?

A: It doesn't, not for long. Again, an execution is such an antiseptic thing, over so quickly and with a minimum of fuss, that a day or two later it is practically forgotten and the men are back to rapping about football, or whatever is in season. I don't think there is a man on Death Row who really believes he'll be executed, who can picture himself walking into the back room.

Q: What do they think, that they are going to win new trials?

A: A lot of them think that, but most seem to think the public is turning against capital punishment, that it will somehow be abolished or modified. Others feel the public would not stand for the mass executions that could follow if the Supreme Court rejects the pending appeals testing the constitutionality of the death penalty.

Q: Do you agree with them?

A: Not for a minute. There are somewhere near six hundred men now under sentence of death in this country. If at dawn tomorrow all six hundred were executed, the howl of protest from the public wouldn't wake the baby.

Q: You take a harsh, cynical view of the public. Don't you believe society values human life?

A: My view isn't cynical; it is realistic, and it has nothing to do with society's basic decency. The fact is that society, the general public, does not think of itself as the executioner. The state does the killing, not the public, a polite little fiction that enables people to go their merry way with no feelings of guilt or remorse, no real sense of responsibility. The unseen act of killing becomes an unreal act, an abstract act performed by an abstract entity—the state. This fiction actually begins with the arrest and indictment for murder, when the charge is described as an act against the peace and dignity of the *state,* not as an act against the people. In theory, the state *is* the people, but who these days thinks of it that way? Nowadays, government is looked upon as an albatross around the people's neck rather than as the servant of the people. But that's another subject.

Q: Let's get back to capital punishment. Do you think the public would feel differently about the death penalty if everyone felt a sense of personal responsibility when the state put a man to death?

A: I think people would be less complacent. It might be that the quickest way to abolish capital punishment would be to make all executions public, then go out on the day the execution is to take place and randomly select someone off the street to come in and pull the switch.

Q: Some people suggest that capital punishment should be abolished because of the danger of executing an innocent man. Do you think innocent men have been executed?

A: Of course they have. It's inevitable. The system is made up of people, and people are not infallible. Even if we could refine the system until it was 99.9 percent free of error, you would sooner or later, somewhere along the line, kill an innocent man, or two, or three, or who knows how many? The only certainty would be that the number of innocent men executed would be less than the number of men claiming to be innocent.

Q: But it is less likely today, when men have many more appeals available, isn't it?

A: No. Once a man is convicted, the appeals courts only want to know if the police and court and jury followed all the rules in convicting him. In theory, if all nine justices of the Supreme Court believed a man to be innocent, but could find no legal error in his conviction, it would be their duty to let the conviction stand. In actual practice, however, they would find a way to bend a few precedents and order a new trial.

Q: Let's talk about your own case. You have long protested your innocence, yet you were found guilty by a jury after an exceedingly short period of deliberation—

A: About two hours, with a lunch break thrown in.

Q: Yes, And since your conviction you have consistently failed to win the appeals court to your side. How do you account for this?

A: First of all, the jury convicted me because it thought I was guilty. The appeals court has denied me because they have not agreed that there was legal error in my arrest and conviction. That differentiation must be made. At no point has my guilt or innocence been at issue on appeal. Some people mistakenly think that the loss of an appeal reinforces the jury's findings, that the appeals court agrees with the jury.

Q: All right, let's take the jury verdict first. If you are innocent, how is it you were found guilty?

A: It's very simple. Based upon the facts before the jury, and the inferences the law permitted the jury to draw from those facts, it appeared I was guilty. I don't think I can blame the jurors for the way they voted, and I cannot state unequivocally that, had I been on the jury and subjected to the same pressures, I would have voted any differently. There was a great deal of circumstantial evidence against me, and my lawyers simply did not have the time or money to prepare an adequate refutation of that circumstantial evidence. And of course cooperation was non-existent.

Q: What sort of cooperation?

A: Witnesses refused to talk to my attorney, often at the urging of the prosecutor—that's standard practice, a problem every defendant has to live with. For example, prior to my trial, and until his death many years later, the county medical examiner refused to discuss with my lawyers the matter of time of death, a key issue in my case. He told my lawyers he couldn't talk to them without the prosecutor's permission, and *that* was never forthcoming. It was so bad that my lawyers had to find a newspaper reporter to tell them exactly where the body had been found. And as for my statements to the police, the first time my lawyers saw them was when they were offered in evidence at the trial.

Q: Couldn't you have asked the court for assistance in gaining the information you needed to defend yourself?

A: Sure—provided we wanted to drop everything else to prepare the necessary formal applications, serve them on the prosecutor, give him time to reply, then go through whatever formal court hearings the judge might have felt were necessary. With only a few weeks to prepare for trial, and the state pressing for a quick trial, you can't afford to waste time on formalities. That's what the prosecutor wants you to do. I don't think the average person has any idea of how difficult it is for someone charged with a crime to defend himself, the enormous disadvantages he has to live with. The prosecutor has all the aces—unlimited manpower and money, and access to every sort of expert assistance from the top psychiatrists to the facilities of the FBI crime lab. Only the rich defendant can compete with that, therefore only the rich have a fair chance. The average defendant must make do with an overworked public defender and, if he is lucky, one investigator. That's the adversary system, and it stinks.

Q: How do you feel about the judge's handling of your trial?

A: Like every defendant who is convicted, I thought the judge was a prejudiced sonofabitch, but as time went by after the trial and I began to take a more rational, mature look at what happened, I saw that the judge had done his best, what he thought was right. I think it was his first major trial, and he was under a great deal of pressure from the press and public. I would have no hesitation about being tried before him again.

Q: How about the prosecutor? Do you feel the same way about him?

A: I have mixed feelings about him, personal feelings, but I recognize that he, too, was doing his job under pressure, doing the job the press and public wanted him to do.

Q: In your first book, *Brief Against Death,* you were critical of the press coverage of your case. What exactly is your complaint about the press?

A: The testimony of the prospective jurors, when they were being examined, tells the story. Of those asked if they had followed the pretrial press coverage of the case, 40.4 percent testified that they had been prejudiced *by the press coverage* to the degree that they could no longer render a fair verdict. That's indicative of the sort of coverage my case received. The local newspapers put together a record of accuracy and veracity indistinguishable from that of the Central Committee of the Communist Party. If facts were dollars, the local press would have gone the way of the Penn Central.

Q: What are your feelings regarding the appellate courts?

A: The early decisions on my appeals, those of the first couple of years, blew my mind. But again, looking back with the perspective of maturity and experience in legal matters, I can see how the courts reached the conclusions they did. I don't like it any better, but I can understand it. The most recent decisions on my appeals have been another matter.

Q: You seem displeased with the manner in which the courts have handled your case in recent years.

A: If I had to, I could write a book—and I probably will. For years, since 1965 on the latest appeal, I tried to get the federal court in New Jersey to hold a *habeas corpus* hearing in my case, an evidentiary hearing at which *all* the facts of my arrest and interrogation could be put on the record, facts such as the denial of my requests for an attorney, the taking of my wife into custody so that she couldn't comply with my request that she contact an attorney for me, the refusal to release her until I had given the police a statement, the fact that I was stripped naked and interrogated in that condition, and a number of other things, all pretty much standard police practices, relevant to the legality of my conviction.

Q: And the courts have refused you that hearing?

A: Consistently, and often without even hearing my lawyer's arguments. Most of the refusals were on narrow technical grounds. In November 1968, the Supreme Court finally ruled in my favor eight to one and said I am entitled to be heard. The case was remanded to the lower courts for the hearing that even the prosecutor seemed to agree had to be held.

Q: Didn't the federal court deny that appeal a few months ago?

A: Hell, no! After making me wait for eighteen months, hearing many many other cases while insisting that no judges were available to hear my case, the court finally agreed to hear oral arguments on a very limited issue, a part of the whole appeal. Had the court ruled in my favor on that issue, the full hearing could have been avoided. The court ruled against me. The judge copped out with the same old line I have been getting since 1965: he said the issue had already been decided—a very strange decision in light of the fact that the Supreme Court sent the case back so the issues could be decided.

Q: What happens now?

A: We waited as long as we could, more than two years, giving the court every opportunity to act, but when the judge continued moving other less important matters ahead of mine, we sought and won his removal. A judge from the U.S. Court of Appeals in Philadelphia was assigned to sit in New Jersey for the purpose of hearing my case. The hearing began three weeks later, on January 18, and is in progress as I write this.

Q: Would you care to make a long-range projection as to the outcome of your case?

A: That's very difficult to do since so much depends upon what the prosecutor elects to do. If I should win a new trial as a result of the current appeal, then the state will have to decide whether to attempt to retry me or drop the charge. Because of the passage of time and the difficulty of reassembling witnesses and evidence, the prosecutor would have a very tough decision to make. Some people have suggested that the state would be willing to make a deal, some sort of deal in which I would plead guilty to a lesser degree of murder. The result of such a plea would be a sentence under which I would be eligible for immediate parole. That sounds very attractive, but I won't hold my breath while waiting for the offer.

Q: How much longer would you have to serve on, say a life sentence?

A: I would be eligible for parole on a life sentence a year from now. One of those strange-but-true facts about my case is that I'm very close to becoming the first person ever to become eligible for parole from a life sentence while still under a death sentence.

Q: You don't think there is much chance you will be executed, do you?

A: No.

Q: You mentioned pleading guilty in return for a sentence under which you would be eligible for immediate parole. How do you reconcile your protestations of innocence with your willingness to plead guilty?

A: It is very easy. I would rather be free than legally innocent. A guilty plea would be expedient, a legal fiction. As things now stand, it's likely that I will spend a small fortune for legal fees, and spend more time in jail awaiting the outcome of my appeals, than if I copped out, as the saying goes. It boils down to this: Do I want to spend a great deal more time in prison before possibly leaving legally innocent and broke, or do I want to regain my freedom in the shortest possible time, leaving legally guilty, but being free, and hopefully with a few dollars in my pocket. I doubt that many people will give a damn either way. Those who believe in my innocence will understand that a guilty plea was a strategic necessity to enable me to regain my freedom. Those who believe I am guilty are not likely to change their minds even if I win a new trial and am acquitted. Such people would write off an acquittal as being the result of the passage of time and my having slick lawyers.

Q: Again, you seem terribly cynical about these things, about the way the legal system operates. Are you?

A: Who isn't, except perhaps those who are deaf, dumb, and blind? My cynicism, if that's what it is, is a pragmatic cynicism, the inevitable result of experience with the legal system, a system which routinely gives a black rapist or murderer the death penalty while most white rapists and murderers wind up with a couple of years; a system which takes a college kid caught with a few sticks of grass in his pocket and puts him away for ten years, provided he isn't the son of a prominent politician, in which case he gets closed-door hearings, sealed court records, and probation or dismissed charges; a system in which a poor slob who hangs a rubber check for twenty bucks so he can buy groceries for his family gets five years, while the corporation bigwig or bank president who embezzles ten million bucks gets a slap on the wrist and a fine he can pay with the interest on the money he stole; the sort of system which encourages prosecutors and defense lawyers getting together over a bottle of beer to buy and sell justice like pork bellies on the commodity exchange. It is a lousy system, the sort which allows the junkies and muggers to own the city streets while the cops are guarding the Russian Embassy or disguising themselves as hippies to infiltrate the college campuses. I have a feeling that if all the undercover cops trying to hustle college kids, trying to sell them drugs to entrap them, were put back on the streets where they belong, it would not only reduce the crime rate, but might reduce the college drug scene to the level of a federal disaster area.

Q: Is it possible you are just bitter because of your own situation, your own experiences with the police and courts?

A: I don't think I am bitter. I certainly don't blame the police for the way they operate. Cops are neither all good nor all bad. The police are a political institution responsive to the public, doing their job as they think the public wants it done, just as the courts operate the way the public seems satisfied to allow them to operate. I really believe that government has gotten so big and independent, so far away from the people, so far above direct public control and influence, that the people of this country have finally said, "To hell with it." People seem no longer to believe they have a voice in what is or isn't being done.

This is no novel observation, that's for sure. The public has for a long time now given the impression it is willing to let the government, let the institutions, do as they damn well please as long as they don't raise taxes too high and don't bug the public too much.

Q: Do you, from where you are, see a solution?

A: I am still looking. I am certain of one thing: We aren't going to find the answers with the Nixons and Agnews and the Mitchell family, nor with the "limousine liberals," but that doesn't mean I've given up, or that anyone else should. Maybe the kids will find the answer. I hope someone finds it soon. A couple of days ago I read in the paper where the deputy police chief of a New Jersey shore town said that his officers stop and search people and cars on the streets late at night because "decent, law-abiding people have no business on the streets at unreasonable hours." That scares hell out of me. When a cop can say that without fear of being lynched, without even a peep of protest, this country has bigger problems than a few college kids breaking windows. People had better start waking up. Today it's only the Black Panthers the police are stripping nude in the streets to be searched. Tomorrow it could be damn near anyone, perhaps those decent, law-abiding people who shouldn't be on the streets at unreasonable hours.

Q: Getting back to the problem of capital punishment, don't you agree that there are men who can never be rehabilitated, who can never safely be returned to society?

A: Certainly, even those who opposed Caryl Chessman's execution agreed that he should never have been set free if his life were spared. I'm sure Truman Capote felt this same way about those two fellows he wrote about.

Q: Are you suggesting life sentences without possibility of parole for those convicted of murder?

A: That's one answer, but only for some people, not everyone. Crime and the people who commit it are so complex, each crime and each criminal a different problem arising from a different personality, that it is difficult to see how there could be one just and equitable solution applicable to every case. And why limit

153

the discussion only to murder and murderers? In every class of crime there are criminals who, with present knowledge, simply cannot be rehabilitated. There are rapists who will go out and rape again when they are freed, and 99.9 percent of them will be freed. It's myopic to confine the view to murder. It's also exceedingly dangerous. The fact is that the odds of a paroled armed robber or rapist killing someone are far greater than the odds of a paroled murderer killing again. People worry about murderers being paroled, but they aren't the ones people should be worrying about. In New Jersey, there is only one known instance of a paroled murderer killing again—he killed his girl friend in an argument—but it's a fact that most of the state's felony murders are committed by men who are out on parole from some lesser offense.

Q: Truman Capote has a theory that murder should be made a federal crime, that persons convicted should be given indefinite sentences, neither a minimum nor maximum term, and that their release should be determined by the psychiatrists and psychologists. How would you feel about a system like that?

A: I can tell you that the men on Death Row would vote for it tomorrow, since each thinks he is one of those who would be released in the minimum time. I've heard Truman discuss his ideas on television. Truman is a nice guy, a very sensitive intelligent man, but I think that when he was writing *In Cold Blood* and researching his television documentary on capital punishment he got to talk to some cute cons who put him on something terrible, giving him a hell of a snow job about crime and criminals, with the result that he has a lot of cocamamie ideas like the one about there being a secret society of men formerly sentenced to death, each identifiable by a dot tattooed under his eye. Nevertheless, his idea of making murder a federal crime and giving indefinite sentences interests me. It merits serious study.

Q: Would it solve or accomplish anything?

A: There would be obvious benefits, not the least of which is that if you had all the convicted murderers confined at one or two locations, say, one prison on the East Coast, another on the

West Coast, in institutions specifically designed for that purpose, it would give the experts, the behavioral scientists, a rare opportunity to study the phenomenon of murder, to learn, if possible, who kills, when, and why. If the problem of murder and crime in general is ever to be solved, we are going to have to start learning something about it, and the place to start learning is from the men who kill. It is a cold-blooded but true statement that each time the state kills a convicted murderer, what the state has killed is an extraordinarily valuable laboratory subject.

Q: And you don't feel a worthwhile effort in the direction of studying crime and criminals is being made?

A: I don't see any serious effort being made. Take New Jersey, for example—a fairly typical state. There are twenty-four men in the death house. Most have been here several years, half a dozen or so more than eight years. None has seen a psychiatrist or psychologist since the first week he arrived, and unless a man bugs out, he won't see a head-shrinker again until a day or two before he's to be executed, when the state will send in the shrink to see if the man is sane enough to burn. The failure of the states to make an effort to *learn* from the men they have confined is a disgrace. It's as if a scientist had a test tube filled with a new and rare strain of some cancer-causing agent and made no effort to study it in hopes of finding a cure for the disease.

Q: It would cost a great deal of money for the type of studies you envision, especially if they were extended to all men in prison, to all classes of crime.

A: It probably would. It might even cost as much as that handful of rocks we got from the moon.

Q: You don't think much of the moon flights?

A: I think it was a hell of a price to pay for a collective national orgasm. Look, if the Defense Department and National Science Foundation can spend bushels of money to study the sex habits of the Costa Rican dingbat, or whatever, we ought to be able to afford a few bucks to find out what crime is, who commits it, and how to prevent or control it. We just can't keep building bigger jails. I mean, it's great when Nixon can boast to the Russians: "The Americans have walked on the moon." But wouldn't it be a lot better for all of us if he could say: "My wife can walk in downtown Washington late at night"?

Q: Would the public support the sort of crime studies you feel are necessary?

A: In letting crime rise unchecked, in failing to seek its roots and causes, the public, whether it realizes it or not, is paying more in taxes and lives and property than a real crime-prevention study would cost. If the president would get on that boob tube he likes to use and would tell the people just what it's costing them in losses and higher taxes each year we let crime go its merry way, there would be a revolution such as Abbie Hoffman never dreamed possible.

Q: Why do you suppose the government fails to tell the people?

A: Because it's easier to run around mouthing off about law and order, conning the taxpayers into believing that if they will just elect Sidney Shyster, just close their eyes to the passing of a few more repressive laws, just shell out a few more bucks to buy the police bigger guns and louder radios, everything will be beautiful. Let me tell you something. In the last fiscal year the Justice Department made grants of roughly $184,000,000 to local agencies. Of this money, about $94,300,000 went to the police for fancier equipment, to study new techniques, and for civil-disturbance and organized-crime control. About half that amount, only $49,000,000, went to improve the prisons, and a mere $10,050,000 went to upgrade the court system. Those are our priorities.

Q: How do you feel about Attorney General Mitchell and some of the laws he has supported, such as preventive detention and the so-called "no-knock" law?

A: Those are lollipop laws, intended to pacify the public, to give the impression that the administration is *doing* something, and perhaps to condition the public to the continued erosion of constitutional rights. We already have preventive detention in the form of exorbitant bail, as unpopular groups such as the

Black Panthers have discovered, and almost any lawyer will tell you that no-knock, forced entry with a search warrant is already permitted where the police might be endangered or evidence lost through delayed entry. As for the attorney general, he's a very important figure. He's probably the first attorney general of the United States to suggest, however obliquely, that the Constitution and Bill of Rights should be rolled up and hung next to the toilet....

Q: All right, I'll change the subject. In view of the FBI's recent report of a 148-percent increase in crime over the past decade, let's talk more about that problem. It is obvious to anyone who looks that our prisons are failing to do the job they are intended to do, and that—

A: That's not so. The prisons are doing a damn fine job of doing what society demands of them. Society demands that the prisons confine criminals, keep them out of society's hair, and the prisons are doing that awfully well. They are not doing a good job of rehabilitating criminals, but neither does society demand that.

Q: You don't think society expects criminals to be rehabilitated while they are in prison?

A: They perhaps expect it, hope for it, but society has not yet demanded it, and until that demand is made, until society decides that confinment without rehabilitation is not nearly good enough, that at best it merely postpones the criminal's next antisocial act, the prison administrations will continue to channel their efforts in the direction of custodial rather than rehabilitative care. Like the police and the courts, the prisons are politically responsive institutions doing the job society seems to want done, as society seems to want it done.

Q: Let's go on with this. Suppose for a minute that you had the authority, a free hand, to make changes in the prison system, to do almost anything you wanted to do—what would you do, and what do you think it would accomplish?

A: As silly as it might sound, the first thing I would do would be to eliminate the word "prison." That word and the concept of rehabilitation are mutually exclusive. A prison is a place

157

where you lock people up, where you confine people for a speci-
fied period of time before releasing them basically unchanged.
It is not a place where you rehabilitate them. I think I would
change the name of this prison to the New Jersey Maximum
Security Rehabilitation Center. By a change of that sort, as small
a change as it might seem, you have begun to formalize your
goal, formalize your emphasis, and make both more difficult to
retreat from.

Q: What would you do after that?

A: I would arbitrarily, capriciously, and without exception
pension off every administrator and guard with more than
twenty years' service, give them their pensions whether they are
qualified or not, and get them to hell out of the system. I would
lose a few good men that way, but more importantly I would
have gotten rid of the old-timers, many of whom have been in
the system for thirty or more years. These old-timers have, for
the most part, penological mentalities that are inadequate in
this day and age, mentalities that make it difficult if not impossible for them to accept radical change. Rehabilitation does not
begin at the end of a blackjack, and neither brutality nor animal-
like treatment has ever made a better man out of anyone. Efforts
to improve the penal system, to reform it significantly, will be
resisted as long as the system is administered by old-timers who
see the reformers as enemies, threats to the little walled kingdoms in which the old-timers are more at home, feel more secure,
than they do in their own homes.

Q: Do you really think the old-timers look upon reformers as
enemies?

A: You'd better believe it. Remember, each time we point
out a failure in the prison system, we are pointing out *their* fail-
ures, the failure of *their* system, of *their* old-time method of
doing business. They feel that any effort to interfere with the
way things have always been done, any suggestion that things
could be done better some other way, is in effect saying that
their past, their record, has been a failure. There are many
like the captain of guards who once told the men on Death
Row: "This is my prison, and no goddamn lawyer or judge is

going to tell me how to run my prison." Hell, there are whole families working in these prisons, fathers and sons working as guards, other sons working in civilian capacities, daughters and sisters and wives working in the offices, all looking out for each other, all covering up for each other. The prison becomes a sort of family business.

Q: It is difficult to see these men having such a stake in what is, after all, only the place where they work.

A: It's a hell of a lot more than that. This place gets in their blood; it's their world, has been for twenty or thirty years, and this is where their friends are, where they feel comfortable. You would be surprised at how many of them come in on their days off, perhaps to take some of their friends on a tour of the place, perhaps simply to *be* here. We have men in here who willingly work the night shifts, who probably haven't slept with their wives except on their days off for twenty years, and they love it. This *is* their home.

Q: Who would replace those you pension off?

A: No problem. In every prison, including this one, there is a small but growing cadre of highly motivated, well-educated, bright young men who have come along in the last ten years or so and are on their way up. Some of the old-timers resent them and refer to them as those "smart-ass college kids," but in a competitive civil service system, they can't be stopped, and they are the hope for the future as far as prison reform is concerned.

Q: Can they accomplish what the old-timers have not?

A: They are a good bet. They will at least have what the old-timers will never have—the support and respect of the inmates. As far as the inmates are concerned, the best-liked, most respected supervisors are, invariably, the "smart-ass college kids." They care, they are dissatisfied with the record of the past, and they show genuine concern for the inmates. The inmates recognize and respect this.

Q: All right, what else would you do if you had the power to institute reforms?

A: I would make educating the inmates *and* the prison staffs the number-one priority, a matter of fundamental state policy.

Every inmate, regardless of his prior educational experience, would have an educational program laid out for him when he entered the system, a program especially designed and tailored to meet his individual needs and capabilities after appropriate consultation and study by education experts assigned to the system on a full-time basis. It would be a program the inmate could, with reasonable application, complete within the minimum time of his sentence, and no inmate would be considered for parole in the minimum time unless he had completed his program or satisfied his education adviser that he had made a genuine effort to do so.

Q: Do you feel education is all that important?

A: Absolutely, and the statistics bear it out. Harriet Van Horne recently pointed out in one of her columns that the recidivism rate among men who had completed their high-school education was only ten percent, while among men who had only a grammar-school education it was eighty percent. Even allowing for statistical inaccuracy, the point is clear. If a man is going to leave prison and compete on the outside, to find and hold a job that will enable him to support himself and his family, while retaining his self-respect, he must have an education. But perhaps even more important than leaving prison knowing more, being more capable educationally, is the fact that study, the acquisition of knowledge, requires a discipline, a *habit* of discipline, that seems to me to be one of the things most inmates lack. Discipline is the key to living within the law.

Q: Can you define the type of discipline you have in mind?

A: Well, I don't mean discipline in the sense that the old-timers think of it, in the sense of a man being a robot, doing what he is told or getting his skull cracked. I mean a self-discipline, a self-imposed habit of doing what one needs to do for one's own good. The man who can impose upon himself, as opposed to having imposed upon him, the habit of discipline necessary to study, to acquire an education, is a man who can impose upon himself the discipline, the self-restraint necessary to live within the rules society requires he live within. Few prison inmates have completed their basic formal education, a huge percentage has never completed grammar school, so that the overwhelming majority of inmates has never experienced the discipline of education, never acquired the habit of self-discipline.

Q: If what you say is true, wouldn't it follow that the act of studying, the effort one puts into it, is more important than what is actually learned?

A: I think that is probably true in the sense that we are speaking here, in the sense that the acquisition of self-discipline is the first priority.

Q: You mentioned education for the prison staffs. What do you mean by that?

A: What I have in mind is neither new nor novel. At the present time there is a minimum education requirement for employment as a prison guard—a high school diploma or the equivalent. That isn't much, not these days. It's probably enough for a man who is going to stand on a wall with a shotgun, but, for those who would be sergeants or lieutenants or captains, it isn't nearly good enough. Under the system I have in mind, the educational requirements would become successively more exacting as a man sought to move up the ladder. For promotion to sergeant, for example, he might be required to have two years of college; for lieutenant, four years; and for captain or deputy warden, he would need a master's degree in a relevant specialty—prison administration, penology, sociology, or psychology. At the present time, the deputy warden, the man who runs the prison on a day-to-day basis, need not have any more education than the rookie guard whose only job it is to stand on the wall and shoot anyone trying to go over. The deputy warden might, in fact, have less, since he would have been hired years ago when the educational requirements were not as great. It doesn't make a lot of sense.

Q: Interesting, but don't you think the prison staffs would rebel at this sort of policy?

A: Some of the old-timers I mentioned previously would object to such "meddling" if they weren't gotten rid of beforehand, but I believe the younger men would understand that the new standards were an attempt to improve the system, to upgrade the job and give them greater reason to take pride in what they do. As I said before, this sort of system wouldn't be anything new or novel. Quite a number of police departments around the country have already put it into effect—some even require a college degree for hiring as a patrolman—and it has recently been recommended for implementation in New York City. I don't see why the job standards for those responsible for rehabilitating the criminal should be any lower than for those responsible for apprehending him.

Q: Where would all the money come from for the things you suggest?

A: I doubt it would cost as much as one might suspect. For instance, at the present time no college in New Jersey offers correspondence education. I believe the state university could easily be encouraged, through grants, to set up correspondence schools that would be available to prison inmates, thereby greatly relieving the need to build costly educational facilities within the prisons themselves. Where prison facilities do exist, the state teachers colleges should be encouraged to grant degree credits to students who would, on a volunteer basis and properly supervised, teach and counsel in the prisons. Such students, again on a volunteer basis, and again for degree credits, could be recruited to staff the correspondence school. As for the prison staffs, the state university could easily set up a school of prison administration, perhaps integrated with the school of police administration, since many of the courses would overlap. There is no doubt that most if not all the money required for setting up the educational system is available from various federal agencies.

Q: Is anything being done today that you would consider worthwhile, with a chance of eventual success?

A: Obviously I am not familiar with everything being done or in the planning stages, but from what I have seen there isn't much to boast about, no fundamental changes being made. Let me give you an example from this prison. For several years the officials made a big thing over the fact that a college-degree program would be set up. That sounded great to the men, and it was *whoopee!* when the program came into being about two years ago. It sounded great, men in prison able to work toward a college degree, but as often happens the fact never matched the promise. Among the first courses made available were Spanish, music appreciation, and art appreciation—three rinky-dink courses that wouldn't challenge a sixth grader.

Q: There must have been a good reason for offering courses of that type. Could it be you don't have all the facts?

A: Well, I asked a senior prison official about it. He said they were "legitimate" college courses. He seemed unable to grasp the distinction between legitimate and meaningful. The inmates took it for granted that the easiest possible courses were offered to get the program off to a flying start, so that the record of achievement would be impressive and reflect favorably upon the administration. That sort of stage-managing for public consumption is what sometimes makes me wonder if the prisons aren't being run secretly by the Defense Department.

Q: So you see nothing hopeful as far as the education and rehabilitation of the inmates is concerned?

A: It might not be all black. They are in the process of building a large new education building inside the prison. That's fine, but one has to wonder if it won't become just another place to teach music-and-art appreciation, just another waste of the taxpayers' money. They love to spend money in these places. A couple of years ago they spent a bundle to build a special visiting area for the inmates and their lawyers. When it was completed they turned it into a storeroom for sports equipment. God only knows what the new school building will become.

Q: Some prison officials have suggested that they have been handcuffed in the past by the lack of adequate facilities such as classrooms, and that once the space problem is overcome they will do a better job of educating the inmates.

A: Has anyone ever known a bureaucrat who couldn't awaken at three in the morning and instantly spout six dozen plausible excuses for almost any failure known to man? Look, the few facilities now in use are being wasted on college courses that help no one. I can't see that having better facilities will in some magical fashion make the authorities see the need for more meaningful education and training. If the authorities really cared, really saw the need to educate the inmates, and were willing to make a commitment toward that end, they could have done more long before this.

Q: For example?

A: Okay, I'll give you a couple of examples. This prison has a barbershop for the guards, a place where they can have their hair cut and their shoes shined for eight bucks a year. It is a very large room that easily could have been converted into an excellent classroom. Next to the barbershop is the guards' tailor shop, where their uniforms are maintained—this is part of the service they get for eight bucks a year. Again, this room would have made a damn fine classroom. Then we go upstairs, just down the corridor from the education office, and we find the private dining room for the staff, where their meals are specially prepared and served. Just offhand I would guess that the dining room could be partitioned into two or three good-sized classrooms. Thus, if the administration were more concerned with rehabilitating the inmates rather than maintaining the guards' little comforts and privileges, space for, say, two hundred or so additional inmates, four or five new classrooms, would be available for the taking.

Q: Aside from education, what other reforms would you institute if you had the power?

A: I certainly feel the state must make a greater effort to insure employment, decent, meaningful employment, for the men on parole. Presently, the state's efforts in the post release area are generally negative, telling the parolee what he cannot do, where he cannot go, whom he cannot associate with. Rules and supervision are important, but the state must do more than act as a watchdog.

Q: What can the state do if employers are reluctant to hire ex-convicts?

A: There are several roles the state can play, but first the state must recognize that just as rehabilitation does not begin at the end of the blackjack, neither does it end at the prison gates. The state must recognize that a steady, meaningful job, one the ex-convict can take pride in holding, pride in doing, is an indispensable part of the ongoing rehabilitation process. With this understood, the state can act affirmatively. An effort can be made, for example, to seek out and educate prospective employers, to make them understand that they, as taxpayers, as members of society, have a real stake in the ex-convict's future, in his success or failure. The state could persuade employers to give ex-convicts a chance, pointing out that an employer who hires an ex-con knows more about his new employee, can make a better judgment about the man, than he can about a prospective employee who walks in off the street and asks for a job. Perhaps, if it is deemed necessary, the state could offer the employer some sort of warranty bond against losses resulting from the ex-convict's possible misconduct.

Q: Doesn't the state already make an effort to assist ex-convicts in finding employment?

A: Sort of. It's a halfhearted effort, a demi-effort. The problem is the state's attitude. Let's suppose you were a prospective employer and the state told you, "Look, we have an ex-con who needs a job. We won't hire him. We don't want any part of our ex-cons working for us, but we want you to give him a job." What would you do? How anxious would you be to hire the man?

Q: Are you saying the state should set an example by taking the lead in hiring ex-convicts?

A: Either that or act as a back-up, an employer of last resort when employment in the private sector can't be found for the ex-convict. There are many state jobs with the roads department, the fisheries and forests departments, the parks commissions, various maintenance jobs, where no great trust is required, where the fact of a criminal record shouldn't be a bar. In refusing to hire its own ex-convicts, the state is admitting that it doesn't trust them, doesn't trust its own efforts at rehabilitation, doesn't really believe that a man who has paid his debt to society should be given a fresh start in life. That lack of trust is not likely to inspire confidence in private employers.

Q: Wouldn't some of the things you suggest require changes in state laws?

A: The state makes the laws, it can change them. . . .

Q: There are a number of organizations made up of ex-convicts—the Fortune Society is one—which purport to help ex-convicts adjust to freedom, to assist them in getting started on the outside. What sort of reputation do such groups have among prisoners?

A: My only knowledge of the Fortune Society, the one you mention, is from what I hear and read. I don't know what good they are able to do, but they are well thought of among the inmates and the younger, more progressive prison personnel. The problem is that *no* organization, however qualified, however sincere in its approach, can do any good unless they are given the opportunity to try. To do any good, to have any success with helping a prisoner, you must begin to help him before he is released, and to do that you must have the cooperation of the prison administrations.

Q: Are you saying the administrations are not cooperating?

A: Cooperation is the exception, not the rule. There are very, very few prisons—this is not one of them—that permit outside organizations such as the Fortune Society to have contact with inmates. In some states—New York is one, I believe—the inmates cannot even read the Fortune Society magazine. Prison administrators are notoriously reluctant to let outsiders into their little walled kingdoms, especially outsiders who are themselves ex-convicts. A warden is a god, and he lives in fear that outside scrutiny of his kingdom will reduce him to, say, an archangel. He is also afraid that an outside organization will achieve success, thereby spotlighting his failure.

Q: How about yourself? Do you think you are a good risk to be let back into society?

A: I'm not likely to invade Cambodia.

Q: That isn't a serious answer.

A: It is if you think about it for a while.

Q: All right, let me ask it this way—do you consider yourself to be rehabilitated?

A: Judging oneself in any manner is difficult, and answering a question like yours is nearly impossible. If you were to ask me if I've changed, I would say yes.

Q: How have you changed?

A: I think I've grown up. When I came in here I was a generally useless slob, a wise guy, uneducated, self-centered, thinking I had all the answers and not giving a damn what anyone thought. I'm still too much of a wise guy, but since I've now written books people call it wit. I'm still uneducated, but I recognize it and have tried, am trying, to learn more about the world, about myself, and about my relationship to others. I'm still self-centered, but not exclusively. I see that there is more to this world than Edgar Smith, that I'm not the whole apple. As for having all the answers, I'm beginning to discover that I don't even have all the questions.

Q: What you are saying then is that you have been rehabilitated.

A: What I'm saying is that I'm not the same Edgar Smith sentenced to death in 1957.

Q: Why are you so quick to discuss rehabilitation as it applies to others, yet at the same time resist the application of that word to yourself?

A: I do not resist the word. If anything, I resist the implication that could be drawn from applying the word to me. People outside might conclude that a) Edgar Smith has been rehabilitated, that b) such rehabilitation must have been accomplished by the state, and therefore c) the public can sit back and relax because it has been shown that rehabilitation works. I simply don't want anyone thinking that my growing up, my rehabilitation, if you prefer that word, is something the state can claim credit for.

Q: You don't feel the state has helped you to rehabilitate yourself?

A: Not unless you figure solitary confinement under deplorable conditions is helpful. Anything I accomplished I did so in spite of the state, in spite of the roadblocks and restrictive rules which, for many years, denied me access to such basics as schoolbooks, a table and a chair at which I could work and study, or even a ball-point pen to write with. When I was doing college correspondence work back in 1962 and 1963, I was able to do it only because I was lucky enough to have the money to pay for it myself, and when I prepared lessons or took examinations, I had to sit on a cardboard carton filled with *Life* magazines, using the bottom of another carton as a desk. And every now and then the guards would come into my cell and take the boxes away so that I had to kneel or squat on the floor, with balance sheets spread out across the bed.

Q: But things are better today, aren't they?

A: Much better. Now, they only ignore me.

Q: Do you participate in any of the prison education programs, such as they are?

A: Are you kidding? I'm not permitted to participate in anything. They don't let Death Row inmates into the prison programs, educational or recreational. We're not even allowed to attend religious services. Nor are the Jews or Black Muslims permitted to observe their dietary laws, not even at their own expense. If a Death Row inmate wants to further his education he must do so by correspondence, and at his own expense. I'm fortunate in that I can do that, can afford to do it. Most men in here can't. They're given a few old schoolbooks, very basic texts, but no classroom work and not enough counseling to be effective. A couple of the men in here have real talent as artists, but they are so limited in the type of art supplies they are allowed that they have given up, quit, and now pass the time sleeping, watching TV, or reading dirty books.

Q: Don't the authorities encourage men to exercise their talents?

A: Let me tell you a little story to answer that. We have a man in here who is a pretty damn good cartoonist, but he needs professional help with techniques, style, and the proper preparation of his work for submission to magazines. One of the guards who worked on Death Row had a relative who was a commercial artist. The guard offered to arrange for his relative to supply the inmate with books, and even to come in a couple of hours a month to give the inmate some professional advice, some pointers. Well, the inmate asked the prison authorities if it would be all right, and that was a mistake. Not only was permission denied, but the guard who made the offer was transferred off Death Row and has never been back. *That* is how much encouragement the inmates get from the authorities. Who can blame that guard if he never again sticks his neck out to help an inmate improve himself?

Q: What sort or recreation do Death Row inmates get?

A: We have a recreation yard and are allowed out ninety minutes a day. But again, the restrictive rules are there. I think the rules were designed by Kafka. We are only allowed to use a part of the yard, even though it is completely walled in, is quite small, and a guard with a shotgun is standing on the wall. No equipment is permitted, not even a rubber ball to play catch. It is against the rules to tie a knot in a handkerchief and throw that around. One time, a couple of men made little soap marbles and began a tournament. Each man involved lost his yard privileges for five days for having contraband equipment. Another time, a couple of men started a broad-jumping contest. It was stopped. Not allowed. Some other men were raising a little patch of flowers, petunias, perhaps five feet across. A few weeks ago a sergeant went out there with a power lawn mower and cut them down. What the hell, if you begin to allow inmates to raise flowers there is the danger that you'll begin thinking of the men as human beings instead of animals with numbers, and the authorities certainly couldn't allow that, could they?...

Q: Are you optimistic or pessimistic about the future?

A: I think it was Brecht who observed that an optimist is someone who has not yet heard the bad news. Anyone who is optimistic about the future of the American prison system hasn't heard the bad news,

Q: What about your own future? If you win your freedom, do you intend to become involved in the issues, the problems facing the country?

A: I really don't know. I have been fighting this damn system for so long now that I may be all fought out, arm weary, the way a boxer gets arm weary from swinging too long and hard. Then, too, when I turn on my television and hear men like S.J. Perelman say they are leaving this country because they no longer find this society satisfactory, I can't help but wonder if Kurt Vonnegut isn't right when he says that the lucky ones are those who can run away.

Q: Summing up what you have said here, could you very briefly summarize your feelings about all that is going on in the world, your aspirations and hopes for the future?

A: I can do that in one word—Peace!

Byron Eshelman

Byron Eshelman, former Portestant chaplain at San Quentin Prison, has worked more intimately and at greater length with more men and women awaiting execution than any other person in America. Born in Red Cloud, Nebraska, he began the study of law but abandoned it to become a prison chaplain. For three years he was chaplain on Alcatraz before taking up the position as supervising chaplain at San Quentin, where he lived with his wife and two children for nearly twenty years. *Death Row Chaplain,* from which the following is excerpted, was published in 1962 after ten years' experience as spiritual adviser to those under sentence of death at a time when executions were common, when Friday was often death-day at San Quentin. As he stated in that book:

> Being chaplain for Death Row is actually a small part of my overall work as a prison chaplain. Nevertheless, I come to know the men on Death Row better than any of the other inmates except the chapel staff of inmate workers. The reason is that I spend more time with the condemned men individually and they often remain in the institution longer than the average inmate. I consider it a privilege to know these men and I feel it is futile to execute them. To me they are no worse than the rest of us and often I find them to have virtues and abilities above the average. I feel that God lives in the heart of each man on the Row and I meet Him there.

The Reverend Eshelman and I met on the day before his retirement. As he sat in his chapel office and told me about his experiences walking with men on their way to death it seemed that his tired, red-rimmed eyes would at any moment purify themselves with tears. The burden of twenty years of ministering to the spiritual and family needs of the condemned made his shoulders slump forward like Christ dead on the cross. I had the feeling that a deep long rest would be necessary to bring this man back to full health. He is one of the few Christians I have ever met.

Death Row Chaplain
Byron Eshelmann

Only the ritual of an execution makes it possible to endure. Without it, the condemned could not give the expected measure of cooperation to the etiquette of dying. Without it, we who must preside at their deaths could not face the morning of each new execution day.

Nor could you.

No matter how you *think* you feel about capital punishment, no matter how you *imagine* you would face the legal giving or taking of life, you would meet the reality of it by holding tightly to the crutch of ritual.

As a chaplain, you might approach the execution with a certain integration of personality that comes from a secure faith and a philosophy. You would try in some manner to reflect a sense of security in the lonely moments of a man's most profound insecurity. But still you would find yourself a part of the routine, and you would be grateful for it.

This is the way it is for me, even though since 1951 I have worked with human beings warehoused for death at San Quentin, where each year we have the largest gathering of "condemned status" in the United States.

This is the way it was for Caryl Chessman. While we waited together in the Holding Room, he showed me, with almost clinical calm, that the nearness of death was producing no evidence of sweat under his arms or on the palms of his hands. Yet Caryl knew the ritual better than I did. He quietly anticipated each step, and was ready for it.

From the book *Death Row Chaplain* by Byron Eshelman. © 1962 by Prentice-Hall, Inc., and reprinted with permission of the author.

This is the way it was for Barbara Graham. When I compli-
mented her on the courage she was showing, she replied simply: "There's no other way to be." But she, too, knew the
ritual well, and followed it precisely.

Death is a part of life that each of us will face in his own
way, and will help those we love to face. Death in an execution chamber is not so universal an experience, yet each time
the cyanide fumes choke out a life at San Quentin, they seep
also into the total chemistry of human society.

II

Increasingly, I have come to believe that the death penalty is
fundamentally a symptom of bewilderment and confusion in
society. A culture that resorts to the death penalty as a method
of coping with its troubled is evidencing the same desperation,
panic and outrage as the emotionally twisted individual who,
in his instability, kills a fellow human being. The striking
paradox is that in embracing capital punishment as a method
of destroying evil, we enshrine the very same evil in our own
persons as agents of the state and of society.

Our own hostilities usually cannot be expressed against
such authority figures as parents, employers, spouses and
other persons, whom we are "expected" to love or respect.
The unexpressed hostility requires an outlet, and the death
penalty affords a scapegoat upon which we can legally express it.

The methodology of the death penalty gives society a
greater sense of release than the violent individual explosion
that results in murder. While legally, morally and ethically
sanctifying our act, we may be subconsciously delaying the
climax in order to savor it more keenly.

What would we think of a private citizen who apprehended
his victim and informed him:

"I am going to kill you. It may be a year, two years, three
or even twelve years, but I am going to kill you. Meanwhile, I
am going to lock you up in a small steel and concrete cage,
fatten you up and keep you there until I am ready to kill you."

Yet that is what we do when a person has been sentenced to die. Even Harvey Glatman was more merciful. Society is expert at cold-blooded, unemotional, businesslike, professional killing. The death penalty is routine, ritualistic, even-tempered, assembly-line annihilation. The state becomes a legal "Murder, Inc.," serving respectable citizens who pay taxes to get the job done.

A person who takes another's life has first of all had his own sense of humanity butchered. He is medically and psychologically insane, although legally "sane" according to the archaic McNaughton Rule.

After all these years on Death Row, I have come to believe that the only persons the death penalty deters are those who would not be likely to kill anyway. Only rational, mature persons are influenced by common sense and reasoning. Such people do not have to have obvious realities spelled out for them; they have learned the relationship between doing unto others and having things done unto them.

Men and women who commit murder do not have this degree of rational control and integrated comprehension. The nature of immaturity is that one is sitting on a powder keg in his unconscious psyche and has no adequate control over his emotions. His reason and his willpower are his most defective resources. He gets drunk at the most inopportune times, uses drugs compulsively, cannot sleep well, cheats on his wife instead of learning to achieve a complete and mature sexual union with her. He is rejected when he wants to be accepted, depressed when he wants to be happy, worried when he would be serene. Such a person cannot be deterred by a law. A society that relies on such a superficial interpretation of human character suffers from its own character weaknesses and failure to comprehend reality.

There are many correlations between irrationality and a fervent belief in the death penalty. Supporters of capital punishment often manifest rigid, compulsive needs to fear and to hate. Their embrace of capital punishment is a symptom of their own mental illness.

The only deterrent to murder is growth in maturity, in depth of insight and emotional stability. These qualities come from experiencing the bonds which draw mankind into brotherhood and mutual acceptance. Unless one feels this kinship and knows that his security and his salvation is interlocked with that of all other human beings on this earth, he is fearful, defensive and driven to rely on murder in some form—either wishful or overt. The presence of capital punishment in our culture is the mark of hate. It is the expression of rejection, of intolerance, of profound insecurity. The New Testament declares that hate and murder are the same. To have one is to be guilty of the other. The death penalty is sustained by fear and hate; it is murder in the same sense that criminal murder is the product of fear and hate.

The repression of unsavory elements in the psyche of a society of an individual is the rigid character-fix that causes crime, murder and advocation of the death penalty. And the psychology of repression is tied in with the phenomenon of projection. What one dislikes within oneself he denies, and he projects it instead to an enemy-person. In an effort to obliterate something within himself, he may go so far as to kill the external enemy-person. This is always the reason for murder, whether it takes place in the gas chamber or in a dark alley: an abortive effort to remove something within one's own psyche.

Murder and capital punishment are the logical fruits of the nonpermissive approach which is based on disowning a portion of our psyche as intolerable. Any such rejected portion of the psyche inevitably gains vitality in proportion to the degree of its rejection. And it grows until it takes over the personality of the individual or his culture. We become what we fear most to be.

In the twelve years that Lewis E. Lawes was warden at Sing Sing, from 1920 through 1931, he escorted one hundred and fifty men and one woman to the death chamber. His conclusions were essentially the same as I have reached during more than a decade at San Quentin. He put it this way:

Not only does capital punishment fail in its justification, but no punishment could be invented with so many inherent defects. It is an unequal punishment in the way it is applied to the rich and to the poor. The defendant of wealth and position never goes to the electric chair or to the gallows. Juries do not intentionally favor the rich, the law is theoretically impartial, but the defendant with ample means is able to have his case presented with every favorable aspect, while the poor defendant often has a lawyer assigned by the court. Sometimes such assignment is considered part of political patronage; usually the lawyer assigned has had no experience whatever in a capital case . . . .

Thus do we seek to purge the imperfections in our own psyche by executing the outcasts, the impoverished, the rejected members of minority groups, the mental children.

We sometimes seek to justify and rationalize our executions with the argument that a murderer is too dangerous a criminal to be kept alive in an institution. But I have observed that murderers whose sentences have been commuted consistently make the best adjusted and most reliable prisoners. Even without intense therapeutic treatment, those guilty of murder often develop a calm and steady way of life after the traumatic explosion that causes them to kill. Seldom does a person repeat his explosive killing when incarcerated or subsequently released from prison. The late Warden Lawes came to this same conclusion:

"Murderers make the best prisoners. They are the least troublesome to any warden, and often they accomplish a great deal behind bars. I know of none released during my wardenship at the Sing Sing who reverted to crime . . . ."

Political campaigns to abolish the death penalty are not as important as the need to cultivate insights and understanding which eliminate the compulsion to kill legally or illegally.

Wherever killing exists, it must be understood as an appropriate symptom for the psychological immaturity of the killer, whether individual or state. To attack the symptom is only to ignore the deeper malignancy. This is the real tragedy of the

179

death penalty. Any society that summarily rejects any manifestations of its own perversity and deviation derives no insight by which to correct its faults. The society that executes its problem children is destroying its own access to insight and self-understanding. It is indeed a vicious circle that the more insecure and immature a society becomes, the less able it is to face its own weaknesses and the more it must rely on attacking the symptoms.

Killing is always related to symptom attacks. It is always a focusing on an effect as though it were a cause. No murderer ever knows why he kills, and neither does the state.

After all these years of knowing the men on Death Row, it is apparent to me that killing has to do with hostility feelings, and that these feelings are related to the amount of hostility one has received from others. In most murders, the killers are involved in a substitutionary process. The victims are practically always persons whom it seems relatively safe to attack. They are the scapegoats for the expression of hostility that could not safely be vented against the original ogre. But scapegoats are not mere absorbents. They have a vitality of their own and invariably pass on the hostility until it makes a full cycle and returns to the source. So it is with the death penalty.

Criminals are dynamic scapegoats. Each time one is executed by society the effect is to intensify the problems of crime. Crime, like cancer, thrives on the surface attack which is preoccupied with symptoms and the illusory disappearance of malignancy.

Daniel Allen Roberts

DANIEL ALLEN ROBERTS, A-31045, Death Row, San Quentin, California, is considered to be a peacemaker on Death Row. He has been a close friend of Dovie Mathis who introduced us this spring. This led to an extraordinary communication about his experiences in the "realm of the psychic." He is gifted with an astounding prophetic insight, what observers of such phenomena call "the real thing." This is the first time he has put his experiences down on paper. After an exchange of feelings and ideas he sat down one night "with a brand new ball-point and a fresh tablet of paper and wrote until the pen went dry." When he looked up it was nearly dawn. The material which follows is a part of that night's outpourings.

As he said in the letter which accompanied these pieces: "I still find this a hard thing to talk or write about. There has been only one person in *this world* I could ever be comfortable with discussing this. This was a spiritualist medium I lived with for a time. She was instrumental in helping me to understand what I was experiencing and how to develop it further .... She was amazing! Many people beat a path to her door while I was living there. She was known as Mother Collins. She was like a mother to me."

Dan was born in Needles, California, 5 August 1925. "I'm a Leo. Needles is a desert town; a wonderful place for solitude. I've a high school education, taken several correspondence courses. I had a sometimes stormy, sometimes lonely childhood. Been married twice, divorced twice! I have four kids, several grandchildren ... I've been told. Haven't seen any of the grand-babies yet."

Strange Journey
into the Realm of the Psychic

Daniel Allen Roberts

In the little town of Needles, California, where I grew up, I realized at about the age of ten that I was not like other kids.

I didn't particularly care for the games they played, nor did I care for their company. I enjoyed being alone. Sometimes, I had my favorite sister tagging along with me when I went on some of my excursions in the desert. I didn't mind her; she was a lot of fun and she seemed to understand me. I also had my most prized possession, an undetermined breed of dog. Now that I look back at it, he was some kind of dog! To me, though, he was beautiful.

When school was out for the summer, I would often take walks into the desert or to the river with my dog always tagging along. We were inseparable. I would have let him in the house to sleep with me if I could have sneaked him past mom. The Colorado River ran through Needles. I had a favorite spot that my dog and I would always go to. We had to do this without the knowledge of my mother; she was deathly afraid of that river, so many people had drowned in it each summer. Wimpy, my dog, and I would sit for hours in the cool shade on the bank. I would talk to him and he would sit by my side looking up in my face as though he could understand everything I said . . . . Sometimes, I think he did.

Then I was hit right between the eyes with one of the darkest days of my young life. I got up one morning and found my dog gone. I never saw him again. I remember for days I hiked through the desert and all the other places we had been together. He was nowhere to be found. I went to the Indian village looking for him. They had given him to me and I figured maybe one of my little Indian friends had decided he wanted him back. I was a very unhappy youngster.

I went daily to our spot on the river hoping that Wimpy would show up. I hadn't cried because my old man had told me men don't cry. But the last trip I made to our spot, I was feeling extremely hurt about the loss of my friend. I sat down and stared across the river to the Arizona side. The tears streamed down my face and no matter how hard I tried, I couldn't stop them. I gave in completely to the self-pity and heartbreak I felt.

It was then I heard the voice. It was clear as a bell. I couldn't locate it at first; it seemed to be coming from all directions at once—which was astounding when you consider that those days the Colorado River actually roared so loud that a person not accustomed to the sound would have trouble sleeping.

I can recall vividly that a strong desert wind had been blowing then too; you could hear it clearly mingled with the roar of the river. But when I heard that voice there was not a branch moving on the mesquite trees along the bank, nor was there the slightest sound coming from the river. I could see the turbulence of the water clearly, but I heard no sound. I had a sudden feeling of fear. It was as though I had suddenly lost my hearing . . . not a whisper of sound . . . just that clear, gentle voice. I remember trying to get to my feet to run . . . . That voice again.

For the first time I could make out the words, "Don't cry for your friend . . . he is happy . . . he loves you, and he is always near you." This really got to me. I saw no one, and made a desperate effort to get to my feet. I couldn't move a muscle! "Don't be afraid . . . I'm your friend; I won't harm you . . . here, see; here I am . . . look at the water." I looked, and there about five feet from the bank was this lovely Indian girl. There seemed to be a glow of light all around her. I remember thinking as I watched her, "How come she doesn't go down the river with that current? Why ... her clothes aren't even wet!" Her braids appeared to be hanging down into the water, but they seemed to still be dry!

Sometimes at night we kids, my sisters and brothers, would tell each other ghost stories we had heard, trying to scare each other. I had no firm belief in ghosts even then as a kid because my dad had told me there were no such things. This is the first thing that came into my mind ... this was a ghost!

This beautiful girl must have sensed my fright, because she laughed in a beautiful tingling voice. "I am your friend ... I have always been your friend ... We have had many good times together ... I am here to tell you not to cry or regret your dog's leaving ... He was called because it was his time to return ... You will understand as you grow older ... There will be another dog for you soon ... Take him and give him love as you did this one ... Always remember, the Lord gives, and the Lord takes ... Always trust the Lord's wisdom ... For now, I will be your guardian. You will not see me again, but I will be near you. Never be afraid again."

I remember trying to talk. Words formed in my head but nothing came from my throat. Yet this girl seemed to know all I was thinking, and she answered my questions without my uttering a word. Then she gave me a beautiful smile and faded away. It was only then that I could hear the river's roar again, and see the wind moving the branches of the trees. The wind had dried my tears; for the first time, I was aware of their sting.

I could move again! I got to my feet and ran towards home as fast as I could. I was about a mile or so from the house, but I'll bet I made that trip in nothing flat! I didn't say anything to anyone about my vision that day. I wasn't aware at the time that it was a vision; I didn't understand it, and in spite of the girl telling me not to be afraid, I was.

That night when we were sitting in the yard with our smoke pot going to drive away the mosquitoes, I told my little sister

Bernice about it. She listened, but she didn't understand. I made her promise not to tell anyone. She was my favorite sister and I knew I could trust her to keep my secret. I knew if I said anything to mom she would accuse me of making up stories. She never believed me when I told her things she could not understand. I didn't know until I was grown that she had thought me strange because I would make remarks that I couldn't recall saying, nor know what they meant. I understand now.

I worried about that vision for days. One night after we had all gone to bed and the house was dark, I stared into the darkness until it turned a beautiful bright blue. In the middle of this light, I could see Wimpy, my dog, romping in a beautiful field. He seemed really happy, and I felt happy for him. Then I heard the Indian girl's voice, "See, he is happy; you are happy for him." I heard the voice, but I could not see her. Fear took me again and I pulled the covers over my head. I didn't remove the blanket until morning; I wouldn't remove it even to go to the bathroom. I don't know why my bladder didn't burst that night.

I did not get over my fear from this vision until I told one of my friends, a very old, very wrinkled Indian man that I had known all of my young life. I can never remember him looking any other way—old and wrinkled. He was very active for his age and we spent a lot of time together in the desert and on the river. He taught me everything I knew about the desert. I didn't realize it at the time, but he was a very wise old man, respected by all. I told him of my vision at the river. I remember feeling a little foolish in telling him, but his face was solemn and never changed expression. He listened to me quietly until I had finished. For a long time, he looked directly at me, his eyes looked on mine. I could not turn my eyes away from his. Then, he spoke quietly to me.

He told me that I was a "chosen" one but I would be tested severely through life. There would be much "trouble and turmoil," as he put it. He said that I must be strong; I must always have faith in the Creator of all life. He told me that I had seen a good spirit, what the white man called an angel; that as long as I kept the faith I would be protected by the spirits; that I must never doubt that life was eternal—not as the white man taught in his religion, but that there was no death as the white man taught. He told me that I must prepare myself to suffer greatly in life. He didn't explain that to me; I suppose he thought it was too deep for me to comprehend at my age. He never did talk to me as though I was a little boy; all our conversations were grownup. He never treated me as a child. He taught me to fish and a number of things that my own father would never take the time to do. He always had time for me when my old man would only take enough time to give me a shove and tell me to get out of his face and go play. My old man was always too busy chasing some skirt around town to ever spend any time with me. The love I might have been able to give my father, I gave to this wonderful old Indian. I always took him some of mom's fresh-baked cookies, biscuits, sometimes a chicken or some eggs or a large watermelon we had grown on our property. He lived alone in a mud and stick hut that was built away from everyone else.

When this old man died, I thought my world had come to an end. I felt alone. I couldn't even discuss it with anyone, since most of my family was afraid of the Indians and hadn't bothered to make friends with them. In fact, my mom would have had a fit if she knew I was spending my time with this old man in the desert.

In those days, the Indians cremated their dead on a ritual ground out in the desert. They would hold what we called a pow-wow, tom-toms beating all night with chanting. They would then take the body to the place of cremation and place it on a specially constructed pile of wood and set fire to it. Obviously there is more to this ritual but I will not go into it any further. The important thing is what followed.

My sister Bernice had begged me to take her with me when I told her my plan to go and watch the funeral rites of the Indians. We sneaked up on them using the brush for cover. We got as close as we possibly could without being seen. The

Indians marched or danced around the funeral pyre throwing sand into the air. I remember that the wind shifted and we caught a whiff of the burning. It was too much for Bunny; she crawled away and hid out until I would come for her. I stayed a little longer trying to get a glimpse of my old friend, but couldn't see anything but flames and smoke. Finally the stench became too strong for me. I crawled to where Bunny was hiding and we made our way quietly home.

That night I could not go to sleep. I lay in bed wide awake. For a while all I could hear was my brothers' soft breathing. Then I felt a cold breeze across my cheek and on my ear. At first, there seemed to be a roar in my ear, deep inside; then there was a soft popping noise inside my ear, something like what you experience when you are at a high altitude. I *know* I was awake even though mom tried to convince me later that I was asleep and dreaming.

Then I seemed to see my old friend standing before me, surrounded by a soft light. He came only to the foot of the bed. At first I was frightened, but a feeling of peace and calm soon came over me. I tried to rise up, but he held up his hand to indicate that I should lie still. He talked to me very softly. He told me not to be sad because he had left; he was happy; and I must remember all that he had told me. We would meet, he promised, many, many more times. He repeated his words to me that my future would be rocky, but I would develop the ability to foresee dangers to myself and others; that I must work to help others. I must believe always in the Creator and cherish all life. I should never feel pain at the loss of a friend or loved one . . . .

He told me many things were in store for me in the future. My friend down the street would lose his baby sister very soon. I was to convince this friend that he should not be unhappy for his sister; she would be very happy on the other side. I wasn't sure I fully understood him, but I did believe what he told me.

A few short weeks later, the little girl passed away from double pneumonia.

We went to her home to view the body before it was taken to

the cemetary. As I stood up by the little casket looking down at her, I had a feeling of happiness for her. I heard the voice of my Indian friend in my ear convincing me that she was now happy, that what I was looking at was only a shell. I remember smiling at his words when I felt a jerk on my arm. Mom was angry because I was smiling. For that I received a whipping when we got home. But I did not feel one blow of that switch mom wielded with such authority. So I did not cry out or cringe. This infuriated her all the more and she laid it on harder. But my Indian friend was whispering in my ear, "Have no fear—you will not be harmed." When that switch came down on me it felt as though it was a breath of air hitting me. Usually when we kids got a licking, especially with a switch, it left big red welts on our bodies. I did not have a scratch . . . not one mark!

When we got these whippings, mom used to put camphor oil on us afterwards—to help heal the marks, I guess. Imagine her shock and surprise when she couldn't find a mark on me! She stared at me as though she just couldn't believe her eyes. I noticed a hint of fear creep into her eyes too. I remember looking at her and saying as I turned to leave the room, "Junior's sister is happy; she is with Chief and someday she'll be back." Mom didn't say a word; she just stood there. She came into my room several times that night and stared at me. I pretended I was asleep. She never mentioned the incident to me again.

My Indian friend came to me again about three years later. He said he had come to warn me that much sickness was coming to the town soon; I was to keep close watch on my sisters and brothers and be careful of the children I came in contact with. He told me I would be protected along with my sisters and brothers if I kept strong faith that we would be all well. I wanted to tell mom and the rest of the family but they had taught me long ago that I would be wasting my time. Every night when all were asleep I would creep out of bed, get on my knees, and repeat the Lord's Prayer and ask that all my family be protected. Several weeks later, a diphtheria epidemic hit many of the children in town. No one in my family got it.

I continued to have dreams throughout my teens, some significant, some not so significant. In some of these dreams, I had many conversations with strange people—I say "strange," but they always seemed vaguely familiar, as though I knew them but their identity was just out of my reach. I found myself in strange places, too; they also seemed vaguely familiar to me, and I couldn't get rid of the feeling that I knew where I was but could never put a name to it. But I didn't doubt I had been there before.

Some of the people I encountered, even though I couldn't put a name to them, seemed glad to see me. I can vividly recall that some asked me if I had come to stay. The place was so beautiful and peaceful that I would be just about ready to say yes when a voice would whisper strongly in my ear, "Not yet—it is not time yet—you must go back—you have much to do." Each time I heard this voice, I would wake suddenly only to find myself in my own bed.

These dreams have been so real, so vivid, that sometimes I would still be able to smell the odors I encountered; I could still hear the sounds as though they were right in the room with me. Many of these dreams have been beneficial to me. Some have prevented me from making grave mistakes in my life. The only time they ever fail me is when I don't heed them.

On another occasion I was awakened suddenly one night by a dream that had me soaking wet with sweat. It seemed that I was floating around in the air over water. I looked down and could see my mother-in-law going rapidly downstream in fast-running water. How she had gotten into this I didn't know, but I sensed that she had gone fishing with some friends and a couple of her grandchildren. This was not out of the ordinary since anytime my mother-in-law was anywhere near water, she was there to fish. She loved to fish and did so at every opportunity.

This dream stayed vividly in my mind. I knew dreams often foretold the future, but in this particular case I tried to convince myself that this one had been just too far out. After all, my mother-in-law was at least sixty years old; certainly she wouldn't be swimming at her age, especially in a fast-running stream!

Even though I tried, I could not shake that nagging feeling of dread and sadness. A couple of nights later I dreamed of her again. This time she was reaching out towards me, begging me to help her.

I woke suddenly, shaking with a chill. I could not get back to sleep. I lit a cigarette and lay there in the dark thinking of her. She was a wonderful woman and we had spent a lot of happy times together fishing. It made no difference to her that her daughter and I did not make a go of our marriage; she still treated me wonderfully.

As I was lying there, I heard a voice whispering in my inner ear, "You must warn her . . . act now . . . she must not go fishing this year!" I was in prison at the time. I could not write to her because she was not on the mailing list that the prison required of all inmates. I did the next best thing. I wrote to Bernice, my sister, and told her to go see my mother-in-law right away and tell her she must not go fishing that year—not once! I told my sister to be sure to tell her not to think I had flipped, just do what I asked.

I didn't hear from Bernice for several weeks. When I did, this is the message I received:

"Mrs. Willis is dead! She was drowned when her car went off the road and into the American Canal. Her grandson was drowned while attempting to save her!"

I never got the chance to ask my sister if she had given my message. It was some time before I wrote home again, and my sister passed away before I had the chance to bring the subject up again.

We can influence our destiny. This is one of the great gifts God gave to all, the gift of free will. We have a choice. If we choose right, we reap a happy harvest. If we choose unwisely, we suffer the consequences. I know this to be true because I was given two significant warnings and did not heed them. The result has been nearly catastrophic—my life has been in jeopardy for the last ten years! I am not out of the woods yet.

We are tested in our journey through life on this plane. This is part of the evolutionary scheme. Many of us cope with it wisely, and many go happily through life with no thought of the real purpose for which we are put here. For me, there could hardly be an excuse because I have been given the key. I weakened. I got involved with the material world. I was tested and I failed the test. I have been contacted and told that now I am back on the path, and no matter what transpires I must not lose faith again. The next two dreams will show how and why I find myself in my present situation. I foresaw this situation nearly twelve years ago. I had plenty of opportunity to head it off. Through human weakness, I failed myself.

I was working for a labor contractor in Oakland, California, in 1950, driving farm-labor hands to the fields in Cupertino, California. I lived with the contractor and his wife.

One night, I had been out on the town. Around three in the morning I took my young lady home and headed home myself to get an hour's sleep before I had to go pick up the hands and drive them to work. I didn't want to take a chance of waking the people in the house. The bus was parked in front, so I decided to catch a quick nap on the back seat. I curled up and I'm certain I fell asleep immediately. I knew the contractor would wake me when he came to the bus; he had done it before.

On this night, I had one of the weirdest dreams I had ever had. I dreamed that I was walking up the sidewalk towards the contractor's home. As I got near, I heard what I took to be groans and grunts coming from the rear of the house. Curious, I ran around the side of the house to the rear. There, in what I can only describe as a dark-grey light, was a man bent over a woman beating her with his fists. I recall yelling at him and running towards him. He didn't appear to move, yet when I tried to grab him, he just seemed to float out of my reach, laughing insanely. Then, suddenly, he disappeared. Even though he wasn't visible, I could still hear that insane laughter! Then it too faded away.

I turned my attention to the woman. Her clothes were practically in shreds. Her face was cut and bleeding. She made little whimpering sounds trying to wipe blood from her eyes.

I helped her to her feet, getting some of her blood on my suit. I gave her my handkerchief to wipe her face, and took my coat off so she could put it on to cover herself and keep warm. Someone was whispering to me to keep her warm, because she was in shock.

She wiped her face and gave me back my handkerchief. By this time she was able to talk. She told me she lived just around the corner; her husband would be expecting her and she had to get home at once. I escorted her to the house she indicated. She handed me back my coat and thanked me, warning me that I must not admit to knowing her or helping her or I would be blamed for what had happened. This didn't make sense to me and I tried to get her to explain. Then she did a very peculiar thing: she laughed. She threw her head back and laughed hard, pointing her finger in glee. I noticed then that there were no traces of blood on her, no marks or scratches of any kind, though I caught a strong odor of blood that persisted for some time.

I was on my way back to the contractor's house when the man I had seen beating this woman suddenly appeared before me. I remember thinking how strange it was that his feet did not touch the ground. Yet he was dancing up and down in front of me, out of reach, laughing crazily and saying, "You . . . you . . . you!"

Then I heard the woman laughing too. I couldn't see her, but I could hear her clearly. The man danced backward and began to fade. It seemed to me that he was getting smaller and smaller, as though I was looking down a long tunnel instead of the street. The next I knew, the contractor was shaking me, telling me to get up. It was time to go to work.

All that day, as I was making my rounds in the field checking the progress of the workers, I could not get that dream out of my mind. I could not get rid of a feeling of dread, nor did the odor of blood leave me. The odor wasn't as strong as it was in my dream, but it was there. It persisted for several weeks. The dream itself was vivid in my mind; I couldn't shake it off. I felt fear when I had no cause to be afraid of anything; I felt constantly as if I was threatened.

I became extremely nervous after this dream. I wasn't doing my job properly; I had no appetite. I did the only thing I could do; I quit my job and went home to San Bernardino. For some unexplainable reason I just didn't feel safe in Oakland. I had never in my life had this kind of feeling of fear and dread. Maybe if I got around my family it would go away; I should be safe at home. I had no way of knowing I was jumping out of the frying pan into the fire.

Perhaps if I had taken the time to try and analyze my dream, I might have come to a different conclusion or choice as to what I should do. I think that feeling of fear blocked all my reasoning ability. In other words, for the first time, I let a dream panic me. I had a premonition of danger and death and could not cope with it rationally.

After I had been home awhile I calmed down. The smell of that horrible blood left; I didn't have that dream anymore. But I did have another dream which was equally disturbing. I seemed to find myself in a courtroom. The judge was talking to me, but I began to hear his words in the middle of a sentence; I don't know what he was saying prior to that. He was now saying ". . . and may God have mercy on your soul."

I couldn't understand what I was doing here. What was he talking about; why was I in this courtroom? As I listened to him, there was no feeling in me: it seemed that I was numb clear through; no sensation at all. Nothing seemed real; the people in the room, the sounds, my sight, nothing. My vision seemed distorted and shadowy. The singsong drone of the judge's voice was so unreal that I took a harder look at him. Then I knew what it was. I was looking at a man's face, but a woman's voice was coming out of that mouth. The face was evil; the mouth had a foul and dirty look about it; the voice was clear but it seemed to be muted or coming from a distance.

I looked into those eyes; they were not the eyes of a human being. As I watched that evil-looking face, it seemed to change suddenly into a woman's. Her face seemed to contain all the evil known to mankind. The eyes seemed to grow, to bulge right there before me; they turned fire-red. As I looked into them, I could see what appeared to be demons dancing deeply inside those horrible-looking eyes. Then the bailiff grabbed my arm and urged me to come with him.

We went directly to a car waiting for us. Two people were in the front seat but I never got to see their faces. They seemed to be whispering and laughing at something among themselves. I was put in the back seat with the bailiff. We started moving and without being told I knew we were headed for San Quentin's Death Row. As we drove, I could picture the Row; I saw it in detail.

When we drove through the gates at the prison, we went directly to the warden's office. I remember being shocked that the warden was a woman! She smiled, but never said a word. She got up from behind the desk and started walking; the bailiff and I followed, climbing a steep set of stairs that led to the Row. When we got to a big steel door, she knocked and the door opened to a dark, smelly hall. We started walking down toward a very dim light a long way away from us. It seemed the more we walked, the farther away the light seemed to get. We never got to the light . . . . Then I woke up.

I might add here that though I had never seen the Row before coming to it, the way I pictured it in my dream was accurate in every detail! That is, Condemned Row itself, not the entrance to it. To get up to the Row an elevator is used, not a stairway. I know what the long tunnel means, I know what the light means; I know why the light seemed to be moving away; but that is another story in itself. Just briefly: the dark tunnel means that there is a rocky, hard climb for me, that the way is fraught with danger. The light moving away means that there is hope; it is quite away off but hope nevertheless. The light at the end, if reached, will be a clean, new beginning. That light is life itself!

The two dreams are not so easily interpreted. That they meant violence goes without saying. That they were a warning to me cannot be denied. The important thing to be learned is that I had been given the gift of precognition; I had been instructed as to certain things that were my calling to do. I, like so many, elected to follow another path, forgetting or ignoring the job I had to do: an obligation that could not be denied, the payment of karma long overdue. We all have a duty to mankind. I only hope others will find their paths before they are led to destruction. I almost made it myself.

Now I feel that I am back on the path. It makes no difference what happens to me, or, I should say, to the physical me, so long as I never stray from the path again. The important thing too is that I know that I have been forgiven for all my transgressions, and that I have forgiven myself.... Oh, yes, you must be able to forgive yourself too before you can find peace.

"All have sinned...." Jesus uttered those words. Still, He held out His hand to the lowliest of sinners offering love, hope, forgiveness and life. Only man with his false values, his hypocrisy, dares to cut off all avenues to hope, love, understanding, forgiveness, salvation of the soul, the very essence of life itself. Knowing this about man, I still hold to the belief that there is hope for him; that he will return to the intended path; that he will see in his fellow man the love, compassion and understanding that is put in each of us by the Creator and thereby become love himself. Man must come to this realization quickly if we are to preserve this planet for evolutionary progress. If not, total destruction will be the fate of man and this earth. The time is now to stop paying only lip-service to the Creator. The time is now to turn inward and find your true self, become one with your Creator.

One of the most profound teachings of Jesus was the words "Judge not, that ye be not judged." He also taught that before we could hold up the lamp of understanding to others, we must have first a knowledge of good and evil. A mentor cannot teach unless he has had to learn the lesson. By practicing this on this earth there would be less suffering, less strife, less sorrow. Then those words Jesus spoke would become crystal clear in our minds.

I make no claims in this field. I am not a religionist; I have a very limited knowledge of the Bible. The things I know have come to me through other sources, call them inspirational or whatever. I only know that when I listen to my Guide, I am on the right path. I need no further proof that life is eternal . . . I *know!*

Influences on the Human Soul

I live in a section of the Row with about thirty other inmates. I have been here since 13 June 1963. I have had three execution dates in that time. I've only been off the Row about a total of four months with court action. At present I am awaiting another trip to court.

There are about ninety-seven men at present on Death Row. There has been a hell of a turnover of men since I first came up: a large number of the fellows went up for new trials and did not come back. I feel that this will happen to quite a few more.

About the only description for this place is hell! If there is such a place as hell, this has got to be the place.

For some years now I have made a quiet study of the men up here. I find that most of them, at least on the surface, appear to be no different than people one would come in contact with daily on the outside. But there is much, much more under the surface.

On the surface the men have their everyday hangups. Of course, these are more pronounced (to them) because of their status up here. Everything is magnified out of proportion. Little things become gigantic problems. There is no trust of anyone, because in most cases we have been lied to and lied on.

It is said that the "eyes are the mirrors to the Soul." I don't believe a better place can be found to verify this saying than a place like this, where men are under sentence of death. Until and unless some action is taken, these are just walking dead men: zombies, so to speak, robbed of all identity, of being human. There is no light in the eyes or faces of these men; just dull, lifeless orbs stare back at you. Sometimes, however, I can detect what could be the beginning of a spark, as though the soul were struggling desperately to come forth to the surface.

This soul could be brought back; it could be made clean and whole again. It takes love, compassion, a desire to rescue one of God's own. You wouldn't push a drowning man back into the water; you wouldn't cut off an entire arm to cure an infected finger. Didn't Jesus glorify the shepherd who left his whole flock just to rescue one lamb? I believe it is man's duty and obligation to save his fellow man, to heal and repair the spirit as well as the body.

The men of Death Row that I have talked to are not evil men. They are men who I believe to be possessed, men who were robbed of their self-control. Not having an understanding of this, they were and are defenseless.

It must also be known, and remembered, that free will also means that at the time of incarnation one has the choice of who his parents will be, the race he will be born into, the country and the environment in which he will have to work out his experiences and karma. Unhappily, mistakes are made. The wrong parents are selected, the wrong race, the wrong environment; wrong everything! Parents may be chosen who are near stupid, or who have no desire for a child or family life; if materiality is their only concern, they will not have a capacity for love in its truest sense. Picture in your mind what this environment can do to this child! The child will not be loved or wanted, so he or she will not develop the capacity to love or understand love. The one thing *all humans* want and need is to love and be loved. There are many, I know, who will not admit this truth, but throughout their journey on this earth, whether they know it or not, they are constantly searching for love. They will try to obtain it at any cost. This desperate search can, and usually does, end in disaster. A very fortunate few may succeed. They too pay a price!

I could be wrong, but I firmly believe that the one element

missing in the life of each and every man on Death Row is love. I'm not speaking of bedroom love—that kind we have all experienced at one time or another, usually with disastrous results. I refer to the deep, divine love of spirit, two spirits functioning as one complete whole. This love exists; unfortunately, I and many others have never found it.

I often sit and just watch these men. I watch the different changes they go through. I watch, and I feel great pity for them; I feel shame too. Shame because there are other humans who condone and perpetuate hellholes like this one throughout the world. I'm not advocating that there should not be precautions taken to protect others from violent people, that crimes should be overlooked or excused. I do say that every effort should be made to salvage these souls, to heal them, cleanse them, make them whole again. This is what the whole scheme of things is all about. Didn't Jesus tell Peter to follow him and he would make him a "fisher of men"? What happened to that idea?

We in this country are obsessed with violence as a means of subjugation. Violence has become a way of life. No matter what we seek to attain, we use violence to do it. It will lead to destruction; like a cancer, it will destroy us from within. It has already started, moving slowly, surely, unabated!

There is nothing to fear from outside our own borders. Others will, and do, see what we ourselves cannot see, that we will destroy each other from within. They sit back and wait. We will do to ourselves what our leaders claim is our fate from without. Such claims get votes, but our major problems remain. We must have wise leadership, spiritual as well as political, if we are to survive. History has a nasty habit of repeating itself. If we look back to what was the fate of past civilizations, we will find it is not at all difficult to predict our future. Will we never learn? Until we do, we will continue to incarnate into the same conditions that existed at the time of our passing from this plane. We do return; never doubt it!

We don't get a brand-new start as it is so fondly put by false teachers and charlatans. Our karma—personal, racial, and as a nation—must be paid. We will pick up the debt where we left off. We have an opportunity to eliminate much of this karma with each successive life; the lessons must be learned. But, due to stupid beliefs and our insatiable lust for material goods, we are multiplying our mistakes, digging the hole deeper!

You are born with a soul. This soul contains the wisdom of many ages. We need only turn inward to learn its wisdom. We must stop idolizing false leaders who are deliberately leading us down the path to destruction by promising to gratify all our greeds and lusts. We must realize that our journey on this planet is for the sole purpose of working out of the hole our past and present has placed us in. If we are to continue our evolutionary journey, our karma must be paid.

As a result of many conversations with the men on Death Row, I have found that one thing stands out above all others. These men are victims of a decaying society, a fading culture. We have been taught to worship material things; we are made to believe that we are nothing unless we acquire this materiality. God, love, country, none of these matters; nothing matters but material things. There is a slogan going around declaring that God is dead. This misuse and abuse of our God-given free will can only bring on our destruction.

I have tried to show that persons who are sent to Death Rows are immature souls. Generally, their lives have been controlled by hatred, vice, greed, lust, all the negative desires of mankind.

These negative traits are not wiped out at the time of death. On the contrary, when a person is forcibly "jumped" from the physical world, he will more than likely "go over" with an intense feeling of hatred. He will have this hatred and his desire for revenge uppermost in his mind as his last conscious thought. This violent desire for revenge will cause him to be earthbound. His spirit will seek out the psychically unstable and emotionally immature. Since he is earthbound, he will quickly orient himself and will learn that he can influence these weak souls without difficulty. He will seek these weak ones in places of vice, places of poverty, any place that will give him access to the type of individual who will afford him the opportunity to continue his evil vicariously. Make no mistake about this: this can be done through the consciousness of any living person with whom he can establish a rapport, a person with similar desires. He can, and he will, possess this person. Haven't you ever done something that was consciously against your very nature and found yourself shocked beyond words that you did it? If you have, then you were briefly possessed. Fortunately, you were psychically stable enough not to be taken over completely. Others are not so fortunate.... Think about that! When this evil and vengeful spirit possesses some unfortunate individual, that person is capable of committing any manner of savagery and violence. How else to explain so-called senseless killings, mass murders with no apparent motive? It should be readily apparent that when man in all his distorted wisdom practices the so-called legal murder of execution, he only perpetuates what he hopes he is destroying!

All persons on Death Rows are psychically unstable and emotionally immature. Murdering them is not the answer. Mankind only admits defeat and his inability to understand and cope with the problem when he resorts to murder as the ultimate solution. We claim that we are living in an enlightened age. Why hasn't man shown that he has seen the light? Time is running out!

When an act has been committed that is a capital offense, the person should be locked up and treated and trained; not jumped over into the etheric world to become another invisible prowler able to fasten onto a weak and similarly inclined person on earth. Society in its ignorance creates these forces and can only cope with them blindly and ignorantly. Until man accepts the fact that there is much more to his existence than his known five senses he will continue to stumble blindly through one existence after another with very little gained in his evolutionary journey.

To me, Death Row is the ultimately cruel existence. There is a constant battle for survival. The weak, the ignorant, the sick, the poor, the unwanted, the unloved, the minority, versus the awesome power of the state. If one is weak mentally, it doesn't take much to push him over the line of sanity. This is happening now.

I have noticed over the years the mental changes in different persons. They are becoming borderline vegetables. Conversations are more and more devoid of meaning. Attitudes are constantly on the change; you can never know what you will face from one moment to the next.

I personally have no fear of death. I know that it is not the end. This was worked out in my case long ago. I understand.